50 ACTING SCENES FOR TEENS

Cool New Scenes
For The American
Teenager

original scenes by Bo Kane

"50 Acting Scenes For Teens"

First printing January, 2010
Burbank Publishing
421 Catalina St.
Burbank, California 91505

ISBN 0-9841950-0-9

On the cover: Olivia Barker, Shelbi Jonas, Sean Clemmons,
and Emma Marcus behind the camera

Cover design and masks design by **Thomas Cain**

To Denise, Makena, and Austin …

for all of your love and inspiration.

"I love acting. It is so much more real than life."
                    – Oscar Wilde

50 Acting Scenes For Teens

Table of Contents

* Due to the subject matter (a girl's decision to say 'yes' or 'no' to her boyfriend), this scene should be viewed with discretion.

Boy / Boy Scenes

* w/ off-stage voice of Teacher

Single Actor / Off-Screen Actor Scenes

Scenes where the actor is alone on stage or on screen, playing to an off-screen actor / instructor.

Bonus Scene

Commercial Scenes

Introduction

The scenes in this book are intended to be familiar territory for the young actor (in some cases, *uncomfortably* familiar), and to stretch the actor, giving him or her room for interpretation and exploration in each scene.

The themes are pretty universal: schoolwork, bullying, holidays, shyness, jealousy, parent's divorce, dancing, sports, cheating on a test, friendship, and goofing off.

Many of the scenes written for one gender will work fine for the other with a minimum of adjustment. Stage direction and emphasis notes are offered, but can be altered without seriously offending the author (slight offense, but I'll get over it). Props are minimal.

Most of the scenes contain a change of attitude or expression, a pause for reflection. Some young actors like to steamroll through dialogue, so the pauses are indicated. Usually there is a particular environment that also should be included in the scene.

For example, in the "It Takes A Thief" scene with Mitch and Michael, the subject is theft and the setting is a school hallway. We would assume there are other students walking by, and that Mitch and Michael wouldn't want their conversation overheard. So the actors must play that environment: looking over their shoulder, pausing before they speak something incriminating, etc.

The scenes are divided into the chapters of:

Girl-Boy

Girl-Girl

Boy-Boy

Single Actor with off-stage actor or instructor

Commercials

A few of the scenes have more than one boy or girl, so watch your staging. Cheat toward your audience or your camera. Let them see your performance.

The scenes are written in screenplay/script form, and are about two minutes (or less).

ALONE ON THE STAGE

The final theatrical chapter features only one young actor reading with an off-stage or off-camera adult.

Many auditions for stage, film and television are performed with the director, casting director, or reader who sits in front of the actor or near a camera.

So, no matter who the other _character_ in the scene is, our young actor is reading with an adult who may not even slightly resemble what the other character is supposed to look and sound like.

Playing a scene with a bearded man who is reading the role of your girlfriend is a challenge, for both the actor and the instructor, and it helps to practice it.

I hope you enjoy experimenting with the scenes, and play not only the roles that are close to your heart, but also the ones that are wildly different from whom you really are.

Remember: whether your ultimate goal is to be a professional actor, or a lawyer, teacher, doctor, or policeman… **we perform in every profession.**

Have fun.

EXERCISES

Before a big audition or job, there are times when you will rehearse a line or a passage, and you make a decision as to how to play it. And it may be a good choice. So you dive into it, give it everything you've got, and you're ready.

You go in and do the audition or job and deliver the lines exactly as you'd prepared, and it's good. The director sees that you're talented, respects your choice, but then says...

> *"Ummm, how about a DIFFERENT take on it? I'd like to change it just a bit."*

CHANGE IT??!! Oh no!

What do you do? Do you panic? Freeze? Fake your own death?!

No. Because you have an open mind and are ready to try any change they want.

How did you get to such a lofty level of readiness? Practice. You've done your exercises.

There are thousands of exercises that actors use to warm up their senses, vocal ability and facial expressions. Some are very good - the mirror exercise helps an actor stay aware of his fellow actor's actions on a stage. Adding subtext is great (more on that in a moment).

Some are a little weird - *'be a piece of sizzling bacon'*, or *'fall in to your fellow actor's arms so you know you can trust him.* (This example fails largely because not all actors can be trusted. Knowing that, **work on your improvisation skills** so that if your acting partner can't be trusted to know his lines or react in character, you can still save the scene).

Back to the audition: The director has asked you to change how you deliver the line(s).

Here's an exercise that will help: practice the exact same words, with several different tones, body and facial expressions, and meanings.

We can also put the emphasis on different words in the line: "THAT'S what I SAID!" is very different from "That's what *I* said!"

Say the following line   *"**What's going on?**"*   in a

    1)   serious manner
    2)   mean/frustrated
    3)   happy / anticipating
    4)   silly
    5)   curious
    6)   sad

There are at least six good ways to say the exact same four syllables.

Try these lines with each of those six expression and inflection changes:

You what?

Give me a break.

What are you talking about?

None of your business.

What are you doing?

Why?

I didn't do it.

I'll show you.

Wait a minute.

That's what I said.

I did not.

Get out of here.

What do you mean?

Are you talking to me?

You're kidding.

Hey, that's mine.

What Do You Mean By That?

In addition to just adding a new attitude or expression, we can also add subtext. Subtext is defined as "the underlying meaning"; *sub* meaning 'under' and **text** meaning 'the words'. What does the person really mean when he or she says something? What do they want, what *just happened* to make them say that? Have you ever said "What do you mean by that!?" You heard their text, now you want to know their **sub**text.

I also like to use the phrase: text *is what we* say, subtext *is what we* don't *say.*

Take the line: *"This is gonna be good"*.   What if this is what has happened before: the person you are talking to has told you many lies in the past.
OR
What if it's this: the person you are talking to has taken you on many wild and adventurous trips.

See how different *"This is gonna be good"* becomes?

Sometimes an actor is allowed to invent an underlying meaning to a line or passage, to make it more interesting.

For example, I once had a small role on General Hospital as a detective, and my lines to another cop were exposition: *'I'm going around the building to check the back entrance, would you watch my post here at the warehouse and report back …blah, blah, blah.*

Dialogue that I might have delivered in a run-of-the-mill fashion.

BUT … in rehearsal I discovered that the other cop I would be talking to was … a very pretty lady.

So, for my subtext, I decided that my character, Detective McGonagle, had always wanted to ask the lady-cop out for a date, but could never get the courage.

But *this time* McGonagle was ready.

So, on "Action" Detective McGonagle looked into her eyes, and *just as he was about* to ask her out … he didn't. At the last second all McGonagle could do was talk about guarding the warehouse, even though *underneath* those lines he was trying to find a way to ask her for a date. He took a last look at her, then exited.

So, **McGonagle the character** only did the lines that were in the script (which I'm sure made the director and producer of the show very happy).

But the **Actor** (me) used the subtext to make it much more interesting and fun to do what may have been boring lines.

And the expression on my (McGonagle's) face must have been transparent; because the day it aired I got several calls from friends who wanted to know if I was dating that actress in real life.

So, subtext not only gives your character depth and range, sometimes it makes it a lot more fun.

One more thing:

A pet peeve of most coaches is when a young actor skips or forgets a word of dialogue … then completely breaks character and stops the entire scene.

The missing word is no big deal UNTIL the actor makes it a big deal. That actor is so aware of their mistake they want everyone to know, not realizing that the audience most likely didn't notice, and the fellow actors don't appreciate the unscripted interruption.

I was coaching a commercial audition where a little boy, 5 years old, was to look through a kitchen window and describe to his little friend what his mother was making for lunch.

Boy 1:   *What're you having for lunch?*
Boy 2:   *I don't know. I'll see.*

He stands on a stump, pulls himself up to the window and looks inside.

Boy 2 (cont'd)   *She's making sandwiches!*
Boy 1   *What kind of sandwiches?*

Here, Boy #2 **completely forgot what he was supposed to say.** He stared through the window (downstage) for a second, then turned to his little buddy and said…..

Boy 2   *Turkey and cheese sandwiches.*

The other boy carried on, not caring that the actual line **supposed** to be delivered was "ham sandwiches". The commercial audition continued with dialogue about how great the mayonnaise would be. The word "ham" wasn't the most important part of the audition, so the kids kept going and turned in a great audition.

What can we learn from these 5 year olds? That unless you've screwed up the scene irretrievably, continue on *"in character"* and save the scene…just the way you would if you were in a play in front of a live audience.

Or in real life.

Another thing:

… (ok, that makes two more notes, but this is kind of important):

In a cold read audition or rehearsal, try not to bury your face in the page. Glance at the script, pick up your line, and then deliver it <u>to</u> the other actor.

Act and re-act <u>with</u> the other actor.

And I can't stress enough the importance of _**listening**_. Maybe you've heard the dialog a dozen times, but listen as _your character_ listens, hearing it for the first time.

In auditions where you have a script in your hand: if you have a long passage that requires emotion and feeling, don't worry that it's word-for-word perfect.

Come as close as you can to the dialogue, and let your interpretation of the character come through.

If you get the job, learn your lines.

Ok, enough advice. Let's get to the scenes and have some fun.

"When actors are talking, they are the servants of the
dramatist. It is what they can show the audience when
they are not talking that reveals the fine actor."

— Cedric Hardwicke

"Do or do not. There is no 'try'".

— Yoda ("*The Empire Strikes Back*")

CHAPTER ONE

Girl / Boy Scenes

INT. CHEMISTRY CLASS DAY

DYLAN is looking through a beaker trying to figure out
what's in it when HAILEY slides over to him.

> HAILEY
> I need to ask you a question.

> DYLAN
> I'll answer it if you can tell
> me what's in this beaker.

> HAILEY
> Iron, you can see it right there.

> DYLAN
> Yeah, so it is. Thanks. What
> symbol is that, F-e? Good.

> HAILEY
> Now, here's my question... Do you
> think I'm fat?

Gag reflex, he almost drops the beaker.

> DYLAN
> Oh no.   No no no noooooo. I'm not
> getting into that.

> HAILEY
> You promised.   Ok, let me change
> it -- do the boys in school think
> I'm too heavy?

> DYLAN
> No. You look fine. Why would you
> ask me something like that?

> HAILEY
> Because I AM heavier. I've been
> trying to lose weight and I keep
> gaining it. I've been exercising
> and eating yogurt and I get on the
> scale and I'm heavier.

He has to think fast.

> DYLAN
> How do YOU think you look?

> HAILEY
> What? I just told you.

                         DYLAN
          No, you told me what the scale
          says. But when you stand in front
          of the mirror in the morning, you
          look fine, don't you?

                         HAILEY
          I don't know, I guess so.

                         DYLAN
          The reason you're gaining weight is
          because you're working out, and
          that's good. Muscle is more dense
          than fat, so it's heavier.

                         HAILEY
          Makes sense, I guess.

                         DYLAN
          Forget the numbers on a scale.
          It's how you look and feel. I
          think you look better than ever.

                         HAILEY
          Really?

                         DYLAN
          Yeah. Simple physics. I'm better
          at physics than I am at biology.

                         HAILEY
          Thanks. This is chemistry, but
          thanks.

                         DYLAN
          You know, Hailey, that was a lot
          for just identifying a piece of
          iron. Don't you think you still
          owe me?

                         HAILEY
          See that? Zinc. We're even.

          She exits.

                         DYLAN
                 (to himself, holds up beaker)
          Dodging bullets and scoring points.
          Who da man? *I'm* da man.

          He writes down 'zinc', then something else inside the
          beaker puzzles him. But she's gone.

                                                    END

                              19

EXT.   LOCKER ROOM DAY

LANA is interviewing CORBIN before a big high school
basketball game.

> LANA
> So, you're 10 and 0, playing a big
> game tonight...is the team ready?

> CORBIN
> I think we're ready, this is why
> we've been working so hard and
> we're gonna leave it all on the
> court. We just try to take it one
> game at a time.

> LANA
> And tonight that game is Highland,
> who I'm sure you agree is not that
> good. Do you think they've been
> lucky, or do they have a soft
> schedule?

> CORBIN
> No, Highland is a really good team,
> so we're just going to try to play
> hard, stay with the game plan...

> LANA
> (interrupting)
> Cut!   Corbin, what are you doing?
> You're just giving me cliche's.
> You sound like Nuke Laloosh in Bull
> Durham.

> CORBIN
> Who?

> LANA
> Never mind. Can't you give me
> something controversial? Say
> something that will excite the fans
> and make them want to see this
> game.

> CORBIN
> I don't want to give the other team
> bulletin-board material. And, we
> really do take it one game at a
> time.

> LANA
> Thrilling. (more)

                    LANA (Cont'd)
How about you say that Highland
players don't have the guts to play
you man to man?

                    CORBIN
Nah, Coach wouldn't like that.
(Pause) Okay, I have something.
You're gonnna like this.

                    LANA
Great, ok, roll camera.

                    CORBIN
Each and every one of our players
will be giving 110% tonight...

                    LANA
Oh brother...

                    CORBIN
...from the first string all they
way down the bench. There is no
"I" in team...

                    LANA
Cut! CUT!!!...Aaagghhh! I'm
switching to weather!

As she stomps off, Corbin shrugs his shoulders at the
cameraman.

                                        END

INT. STUDY HALL DAY

BEN is working on what seems to be a test. CASSIDY, sitting next to him, slowly pays attention.

                    BEN
              (to himself)
          Let's see, the capital of Texas
          is...Houston. Writer of the
          Declaration of Independence: …
          George Washington. Square root of
          16 is … 5.

                    CASSIDY
          What are you doing?

                    BEN
          A test.

                    CASSIDY
          You know all those answers are
          wrong, don't you?

                    BEN
          Yeah. But I don't want to be too
          far off or she'll know I'm trying
          to flunk. (*she looks at him:
          "What!?"*) Mrs. Harris want me to
          go into advanced class and I don't
          want to go.

                    CASSIDY
          Why not?

                    BEN
          All my friends are in my class now.
          And they sure aren't going in to
          advanced. I'd rather hang with
          them.

                    CASSIDY
          Let me get this straight: you'd
          play up a grade in baseball, you
          tried out for basketball and
          wouldn't quit 'til you made
          first string. You've even tried to
          get to get to the next level in
          every Nintendo ever invented! But
          you don't want to get to the next
          level in life?

                    BEN
          It sounded better when I said it.

                    CASSIDY
You see your friends after school
every day.

                    BEN
Yeah. And I don't want them to
make fun of me.

                    CASSIDY
They won't, and even if they did
it would be out of jealousy. Every
one of those guys wants to be
smart like you.

                    BEN
But what if I'm not? What if I
can't cut it with all you girls?
I'm gonna stay where I am.

                    CASSIDY
Well, I guess Mrs. Harris and
I were wrong. Maybe you're not
so smart.

She gives him an eye-roll, turns away from him with a
subtle "L" on her forehead. He sees the "Loser" sign as
she exits.

He sits, thinks. PAUSE.

Then with a heavy sigh starts changing his answers.

                    BEN
              (to himself)
Austin. Jefferson, not
Washington. Square root is 4.
Too smart for my own good ...
the hypotenuse.....

                                                  END

EXT. SCHOOL COURTYARD DAY

JAKE is studying when SARAH slides in next to him.

                    JAKE
          Hey, Sarah, what's up?

                    SARAH
          Well, there's the school fair
          coming up after the game on
          Saturday. What do you think about
          asking Nicole?

                    JAKE
          I don't know, I .....

                    SARAH
          What do you think of her? Do you
          like her?

                    JAKE
          She's ok, she's nice I guess, like
          you. I mean, she's your friend,
          right?

                    SARAH
          Yeah. What else?

                    JAKE
          Well, she's...pretty. Not as
          pretty as you, but, you know...
          what am I trying to say?..

                    SARAH
          I don't know.

They look at each other, look down, look back.

                    JAKE
          I guess if you want me to go with
          her...

                    SARAH
          I didn't say that, I was just
          asking.

                    JAKE
          Well, if you won't go with me, then
          it'd be ..ok...

                    SARAH
          Are you asking me?

                         24

It's now or never. He takes a deep breath.

                    JAKE
          Yeah.

Sarah waits, moves her hand in a circular motion like "go
on, you have to say it all".

                    JAKE (CONT'D)
          Do you want to go to the school
          fair with me?

                    SARAH
          Sure. I'd like that.

                    JAKE
          Great. Ok. (closes book) I'm
          going to go over to the cafeteria.

                    SARAH
          Ok. See you over there.

They smile. As he leaves, he stops, turns back.

                    JAKE
          Did Nicole really ask you to ask
          me?

                    SARAH
          Maybe.

                              END

LUCAS, MADISON, AND AIDEN   *"UNCONDITIONAL RELEASE"*

EXT. SCHOOL COURTYARD DAY

LUCAS sees MADISON coming his way and smiles big.

>   LUCAS
> Maddie! Hey, I was looking for
> you. Want to talk to you about
> Friday night...

>   MADISON
> Yeah, I want to talk to you too.

>   LUCAS
> Good. I got paid for that
> gardening job, so ...hey, you ok?

>   MADISON
> Um...Lucas, I ... I'm fine, I just
> ... don't think it's working out,
> you know, us....uh...I don't...

>   LUCAS
> What?   Are we breaking up? Is
> that what you're saying?

>   MADISON
> I like you Lucas, but....yeah,
> basically, I think we should, you
> know? You've been gone a lot with
> your friends, ...

>   LUCAS
> I've been working. So that we
> could go out. But hey, whatever,
> if you think we should break up ...
> who are you going out with now?

>   MADISON
> No one!   I still care about you.
> I just think we should ... take a
> break. Ok?

>   LUCAS
> Ok. Ok, I'll see you around.

>   MADISON
> Ok. I'm sorry, I..

>   LUCAS
> Don't. It's ok.

She bolts. He stands there for about 10 seconds with every
possible emotion running through his brain and body.

Then....AIDEN yells to him, breaking his thoughts.

                    AIDEN
          Lucas! What's doing? What's the
          matter?

                    LUCAS
               (rubs his eyes)
          Nothing. Allergies I think.
          Going to the gym?

                    AIDEN
          Nah, I gotta work. Hey, too
          bad you're booked up Friday, I
          got tickets...

                    LUCAS
          I'm not booked up Friday.
          What've you got?

                    AIDEN
          Concert tickets, but I thought
          you were with Madison? What
          happened?

He thinks about telling the truth, then...

                    LUCAS
          Put her on waivers. Gave her
          her unconditional release.

                    AIDEN
          No kidding? Man, I didn't see
          that coming.

Lucas nods his head like "me neither".

                    AIDEN (Cont'd)
          So let's go! Maybe we'll find us a
          couple of free agents!

                    LUCAS
          Let's do it.

Aiden heads out. Lucas glances back to where Madison had
been, and then joins Aiden.

                    AIDEN
          You do have some bad allergies.

                    LUCAS
          Yeah. I do.

                                        END

BROTHER & SISTER   *"VACATION"*

EXT. CABIN IN THE WOODS DAY

TALLAHASSEE and her younger brother DUNCAN sit on the
porch of a vacation cabin, bored out of their skulls.

                    TALLY
          You could have at least smuggled in
          an Ipod.

                    DUNC
          Wouldn't have done ME any good;
          you'd just listen by yourself. I
          brought a football.

                    TALLY
          Yeah thanks.

They sit with their chins in their hands.

                    DUNC
          Do you ever wish you had a sister
          instead of a brother?

                    TALLY
          Duh....yeah! Someone I could shop
          for clothes with, someone who
          understands me? Someone who
          would've brought an Ipod? Yeah.
          Why? Don't you wish you had a
          brother instead of me?

                    DUNC
          No.

Pause. Tally sees that she's hurt her brother's feelings,
and then suddenly laughs out loud.

                    TALLY
          HA-HA. Gotcha! You thought I was
          serious!

                    DUNC
          You were.

                    TALLY
          No I wasn't. I wouldn't trade you
          for anybody. If I had a sister I'd
          have to share my clothes with her,
          and my hairbrush-yick! I'd always
          be compared to her in dance
          class...no way. I'm fine with
          things just the way they are.

                    DUNC
          Me too.

                    TALLY
          Come on. Let's see if that
          spaghetti arm of yours can throw a
          spiral.

                    DUNC
          Let's see if those sissy manicured
          fingers of yours can catch one. Go
          long. (she runs off) Keep going,
          go, go, farther .....

     She's off-stage and gone. He tucks the ball under his
     arm and walks the other way.

                    DUNC (CONT'D)
          Sucker.

                                                       END

     "All the world's a stage, and most of us are desperately
     unrehearsed."

                    -Sean Casey

AUTUMN & ZAK   *"HENDRIX' GUITAR"*

INT. LIVING ROOM   DAY

ZAK and AUTUMN walk into Zak's house when he sees the big
box on the couch…

                    ZAK
          Alright! It's here!

As he tears open the box...

                    AUTUMN
          What is that?

                    ZAK
          Only an official, vintage,
          psychedelically-cool Jimi Hendrix
          guitar!

He pulls out the guitar and holds it up.   At first Autumn
looks quizzical, then laughs.

                    AUTUMN
          You're kidding, right?

                    ZAK
          Does this look like I'm kidding?

He winds up and twangs the strings….

                    ZAK (CONT'D)
          'Scuse me, while I kiss the sky!
          Bwang bwang bwang....ba ba bum...

                    AUTUMN
          Uh, Zak? Jimi? Where did you get
          that ... vintage guitar?

                    ZAK
          Craig's List.   I can't believe the
          guy let it go for only 300 bucks.
          Some people are just morons.

                    AUTUMN
          Yeah, they sure are.   And some of
          those morons buy little girls'
          guitars.

He stops playing.

                    ZAK
          Say what?

                                30

                    AUTUMN
          I don't know who Hendrix is, but
          THAT is a little girls' Daisy Rock
          guitar.

                    ZAK
          You are so wrong!   This is totally
          a guy's guitar. Plus, I saw this
          guitar in the famous Hendrix poster
          with butterflies! Look at it!

Autumn turns the guitar over and sees a name carved on the
back.

                    AUTUMN
          Well, unless Hendrix' nickname is
          "Missy Sue", you're not just gonna
          "kiss the sky", you're gonna kiss
          your money good-bye.

She laughs as she heads to the door. He turns it over and
reads the 'Missy Sue'.

                    ZAK
          No.   I did not just pay 300
          dollars for a girls' guitar.

                    AUTUMN
          Maybe you can take your little
          Daisy guitar and play with the
          "Pussycat Dolls."

She laughs heartily as she exits. He stands alone with the
guitar.

                    ZAK
          I hate Craig.

                                        END

[Note: the prop could be an actual Daisy Rock guitar, or any
guitar with a butterfly sticker on it. "Purple Haze © Jimi
Hendrix. Check it out.]

                          31

INT. STUDY HALL DAY

TIA is reading a book when AARON walks up.

> AARON
> What are you doing?

> TIA
> Reading. Obviously.

> AARON
> Reading what?

> TIA
> A book. "Of Mice And Men".

> AARON
> You're reading a book about mice?

Tia puts the book down, turns to him.

> TIA
> No, it's Steinbeck. It's a
> classic. Haven't you ever read a
> book?

Aaron thinks about it for a second...

> AARON
> Do comic books count? (*she glares
> at him*) Then no. Not a book that
> I wasn't forced to read. And even
> then I don't think I ever finished
> one.

> TIA
> So the only life you've ever
> explored is your own. That's
> pretty pathetic. Here, take this.

> AARON
> I don't like reading books.

> TIA
> Yes you do, you just don't know it
> yet. You'll go places and feel
> things, explore a different world.
> It's a good book, read it.

> AARON
> I, uh, really...ok.

                    TIA
          Trust me. Read. Before your brain
          turns to jello.

She leaves.

                    AARON
               (to himself)
          Ok. You want me to read a book
          about mice, I'll read a book about
          mice. Maybe they're mutant ninja
          mice. What's wrong with jello?

                                             END

*"I know that if I can't move people, I have no business
being an actor."*

                    - Alan Arkin

INT. STUDY HALL DAY (THREE DAYS LATER)

Aaron is reading a book, with a stack of other books next to
him. Tia slides in next to him.

            TIA
    Hey, bookworm. Learning anything?

            AARON
    All kinds of stuff! Did you know
    that Velcro was invented by a Swiss
    guy who got burrs on his socks when
    he was walking through the woods?
    And that Benjamin Franklin invented
    the rocking chair?

            TIA
    That's, uh...good. Have you been
    doing any homework, or reading any
    of your assigned books?

            AARON
    Nah, but you know what? Mark Twain
    never graduated from grade school.
    And he did all right. You know
    what else? Starfish don't have
    brains. Guess that explains
    Patrick on Spongebob.

            TIA
    Speaking of brains, these books are
    good, and I'm glad you're reading,
    but they're just facts. You need
    to read some history, math...you
    know, problem-solving.

            AARON
    Hey, Thomas Edison was afraid of
    the dark, so he invented the light
    bulb. That's what I call problem-
    solving.

            TIA
    Ooo-kay. Read what you want, I'm
    just glad you're reading. But, we
    have a test in geography today.

            AARON
    I'm ready. Did you know that
    Vermont has the only state capital
    that doesn't have a McDonald's in
    the whole city?

                    TIA
          Did you know that that city is
          Montpelier? Come on, let's go to
          class.

As they exit...

                    AARON
          Maine is the only state that has
          only one syllable in its name.

                    TIA
          Great.

                    AARON
          And a rat can go without water
          longer than a camel.

                    TIA
          I've created a monster!

                                        END

JOSH AND OLIVIA   *"CHICK FLICK"*

INT. OLIVIA'S HOUSE   EVENING

OLIVIA and JOSH enter holding hands.

                    OLIVIA
          What do you want to do tonight?

                    JOSH
          Anything you want.

                    OLIVIA
          A movie?

                    JOSH
          Sure. Whatever you want.

She drops his hand and grabs her laptop (or iphone).

                    OLIVIA
          Great! Let's look.   Here's a great
          one, I want to see "The Dowry". It's
          based on a Jane Austen book.

                    JOSH
          Oh no, it's a chick flick. Can't you
          see that with....

                    OLIVIA
          It's got Hayden Pantierre AND Meryl
          Streep, only the best actress in the
          entire world.

                    JOSH
          Really? Was she in any of the "Fast
          and Furious" movies?

                    OLIVIA
          No!

                    JOSH
          The defense rests.

                    OLIVIA
          We're not going to some car-chase,
          fighting-in-front-of-girls-in-
          tight-shorts "dumb-fest".

He pretends to be stabbed in the heart. The knife twists,
and he falls to the floor. She stands over him.

                    OLIVIA (CONT'D)
          This time we're going to see a
          movie with an actual plot.

                    JOSH
          Let me guess the plot: English
          girl without an inheritance tries
          to marry a rich guy.

She is suddenly impressed, then, just as quickly...

                    OLIVIA
          Someone just said a minute ago
          Anything you want. Wasn't that
          you?

He gets up.

                    JOSH
          I didn't know "anything" meant
          "chick flick". Doesn't this fall
          under 'cruel and unusual
          punishment'?

                    OLIVIA
          No. The **prosecution** rests.

She grabs his hand again and leads him out.

                    JOSH
          Persecution is more like it.

                    OLIVIA
          And no Ipod in the theatre.

                    JOSH
          Now we're talking torture. Extreme
          violation of some kind of code...

He continues to ad-lib complaints all the way out.

                                        END

EXT. BLEACHERS DAY

A boy sits alone in the bleachers studying. He doesn't
see a girl approaching.

                    TANYA
          Hi. So you're the new guy in
          school, huh?

                    JASON
          That's me. Hi. I'm Jason.

He extends his hand to shake. She looks at it, takes it
ever-so-briefly.

                    TANYA
          You touched me. That's kind of
          like flirting.

                    JASON
          No, that's kind of like being
          polite.

                    TANYA
          Well, my boyfriend is over there
          and if he saw it he'll think its
          flirting.

                    JASON
          Tell him not to worry. Nice
          talking to you.

He goes back to his studies.

                    TANYA
          Oh, he'll worry.   He gets really
          jealous. You might be in big
          trouble.

Jason sees where this is going.

                    JASON
          Then you'll excuse me if I don't
          pay any more attention to you.

                    TANYA
          Too late. He's already seen you.
          He might want to "talk" to you
          after school.

                    JASON
          You'd like that wouldn't you?
               (he stands to leave)
          Is that the initiation here? Well,
          you tell your boyfriend it'll have
          to be RIGHT after school. I have
          to be at the dojo by four.

                    TANYA
          The what?

                    JASON
          Dojo. I'm entering your local
          karate tournament this weekend.
          Black belts only.

He gets his books, stands up straight and looks her right
in the eye.

                    JASON (CONT'D)
          You're dangerous. You need to grow
          up.

He leaves her standing alone.

                                             END

"It's easy to fool the eye, but hard to fool the heart."

                                   - Al Pacino

INT. CAFETERIA   DAY

Two student "news anchors", CASEY and JULIA, are sitting
at a make-shift news desk over-looking the cafeteria.

                    CASEY
          Welcome back to Lunchroom News,
          where we have a bird's-eye view of
          all the action. I'm Casey McDonald.

                    JULIA
          And I'm Julia Rosetti. Let's go
          live with breaking news: new
          student, sophomore Tiffany Garrett,
          is making an attempt to sit down
          with the "cool" girls, not
          realizing that not only are they
          'too cool for school', but they're
          juniors.

                    CASEY
          And here it comes .... Re-jected!
          With the swiftness and cruelty of a
          dead-fish slap across her face,
          Tiffany is now carrying her tray to
          a remote corner of the lunchroom.

                    JULIA
          It could be interesting when the
          cool-but-cruel girls discover that
          Tiffany is a state-ranked gymnast
          here on scholarship.

                    CASEY
          We'll keep you updated. The
          lunchroom today is featuring a
          'noodle-surprise' dish that
          strangely resembles yesterday's
          Chinese dish and Tuesday's
          spaghetti.

                    JULIA
          Our kitchen recycles all food and
          food by-products.

Julia looks off and sees a student about to make a leap.

                    JULIA (CONT'D)
          Uh-oh, back to live action, it
          looks like Carson Hudson is going
          to attempt to hurdle the entire
          science club lunch table. He's
          making his run, he's up, and ...

Both news anchors wince.

                    CASEY
          Ooohhh!   Just missed it!

                    JULIA
          That's gotta hurt.

                    CASEY
          So what Carson thought would be an
          admirable athletic feat .... has
          become a loud and painful bit of
          comic relief.

                    JULIA
          Guys are such fools.

Casey leans in to her.

                    CASEY
          Uh, Julia, we're journalists.   That
          was commentary.

                    JULIA
          That wasn't commentary. That's a
          known fact. (to camera) That's
          all for Lunchroom News, I'm Julia
          Rossetti.

                    CASEY
          And I'm Casey McDonald. Thanks for
          watching. See you tomorrow.

                                        END

EXT. SCHOOL HALLWAY DAY

Two girls, GABRIELLE and TARA, are having an animated discussion while walking to class.

> GABRIELLE
> ...I even stood right behind him, my back to his, like this, while he was talking to his coach. So, no matter which way he turned around and walked, he would bump into me, and we would talk.
> Good idea, right?

> TARA
> So? What happened?

> GABRIELLE
> He never turned around. He walked straight ahead into the coaches' office and didn't even know I was there.

> TARA
> Well, Prom is in six weeks, you better think of something. I know! He drives that old Chevy. We'll let the air out of his tires, then you drive up, you just happen to have a pump....

> GABRIELLE
> No! I'm not doing that, are you crazy?

> TARA
> Yeah, I'm too crazy. So go ahead and think of something, 'cause here he comes.

> GABRIELLE
> What?

> TARA
> He's walking right toward you, Smart Girl. Do something.

Gabrielle turns to see AJ walking toward them. She's flustered for a moment, then FALLS TO THE FLOOR right in front of him.

42

                    GABRIELLE
          AHHH! Ow, my ankle.

                    AJ
          Hey, are you all right?

                    GABRIELLE
          It's my ankle, I think I twisted
          it. Can you help me up?

                    AJ
          Sure. Maybe you need to see the
          nurse; do you think you can make
          it?

                    TARA
          No! No, she can't! It might be
          broken. I'd take her, but you're
          so much stronger, and more ....
          stronger. And the nurse's office
          is way over...(looks around) a long
          way.

                    AJ
          Actually it's just across the hall.
          Here, Gabby, put your arm over my
          shoulder.

                    GABRIELLE
          Oh, thank you AJ. I'm not too
          heavy for you, am I?

                    AJ
          Nah. Light as can be. You ok?

                    GABRIELLE
          Feeling a lot better. Thanks.

As she limps along with him toward the nurses office, she
gives Tara a surreptitious 'thumbs up'. Tara rolls her
eyes, smiles, shakes her head as she exits....

                    TARA
          Guys are so easy.

                                        END

Scene Notes:

In "*Chemistry and Self Esteem*" Dylan can be a bright, intuitive guy who just doesn't study. Playing him 'dumb' might not be the best choice; he obviously can think on his feet.

What kind of "comic moment" does he exhibit after her initial question? Almost drop the beaker? Gag? Boingy-eyed look of desperation?

Does Hailey feel good about herself and her shape when she leaves? How does she (subtly) show that?

In "*The Sports Reporter*" Lana is ambitious, driven, and not very tolerant, but don't forget: she's also funny.

At the end of "*All's Fair*", once Jake discovers that Sarah "worked him" to get him to ask her to the fair, does he admire her cleverness, or know that he has to keep his guard up? Or both? How does he show that?

In "*Unconditional Release*", there is a pause before Lucas lies to Aiden about what just happened with Maddie. Be sure to play that brief moral dilemma.

In "*Hendrix' Guitar*" Zack is stoked at the beginning of the scene. As he discovers the truth, does he *slowly* realize it, or does it hit him suddenly like a brick to the head? You choose.

Autumn's obvious choice is to be a snotty know-it-all. What's a not-so-obvious choice?

Scene Notes

In the second _"Fun-damental Reading"_ scene, Aaron is excited about his new-found knowledge; a complete turn-around. It's this second scene that gives an actor a clue as to how to play the first _"Fun-damental"_ scene.

In _"Chick Flick"_ Josh has a good bit of physical comedy. It's not shtick, its physical comedy. Have fun with it.

Same with Gabrielle in _"Falling For A Guy"_. It's your own version of Lucy Ricardo, Laverne & Shirley, or Maddie from Zack & Cody. Have fun doing this pratfall and all of the physical comedy.

"Why are you trying so hard to fit in when you were born to stand out?"

   - from the movie "What A Girl Wants"

45

"Acting is all about honesty.   If you can fake that, you've got it made."

— George Burns

CHAPTER TWO

Girl / Girl Scenes

MAKENNA AND HANNAH   *"CUE THE ACTOR"*

INT. STAGE   DAY

MAKENNA and HANNAH are rehearsing.   Makenna begins 'in character' as the murder suspect.

> MAKENNA
> (in character)
> *"I was not in the room, I was in the kitchen. Therefore, the murder must have occurred in either the study or the foyer."*

> HANNAH
> *"But the body was ... the body"* ... wait, you were supposed to say the foyer or the study, not the other way around.

> MAKENNA
> What difference does it make? Keep going. We only have a few minutes to rehearse.

> HANNAH
> The DIFFERENCE is that it was my cue. You gave me the wrong cue.

> MAKENNA
> If you had been "in character" it wouldn't have mattered.

> HANNAH
> I WAS in character. YOUR character gave me the wrong line.

> MAKENNA
> How does "your character" know what the line is going to be?!

> HANNAH
> Look, if you can't play it the way it's supposed to...

> MAKENNA
> If you can't act your part...

Both start to argue at the same time…

> HANNAH
> Maybe you should just learn your lines!

48

MAKENNA
Why don't you worry about your
own?!

HANNAH
I'm trying to! Leave me alone!

MAKENNA
I can't I have to work with you!

HANNAH
Maybe you don't!

MAKENNA
Oh, so now you're quitting?

HANNAH
No, I'm not. Lucky for me, my
"character" doesn't like you
anyway.

MAKENNA
Lucky for you.

Pause.

MAKENNA (Cont'd)
I'll try to say foyer first, your
Highness.

HANNAH
I don't care what you say, I'm
going with it.   Toad.

MAKENNA
Whiner.

HANNAH
Diva.

They stop, stare at each other for a moment.

MAKENNA
This is good, this is where we're
supposed to be.

HANNAH
Yeah. I feel it. This is the way
my character is supposed to feel.

MAKENNA
Good. We'll argue before every
show.

HANNAH
Uhh, maybe we could just remember
this one over and over again.

                    MAKENNA
          Ok. Let's rehearse on the way back
          to class.

They walk off.

                    HANNAH
          There's a name for that kind of
          acting, but I can't remember what
          it is.

                    MAKENNA
          Me neither.

                                        END

*"The scenery in the play was beautiful, but then the
actors got in front of it."*

                    — Alexander Woollcott

"You've got to be original, because if you're like someone else, what do they need you for?"

— Bernadette Peters *(Inside the Actors Studio)*

EXT. BENCH NEAR SCHOOL DAY

SAMANTHA sits alone on a bench as AMY approaches.

>   AMY
> Hey, I heard about what happened.
> You ok?

>   SAM
> No. I'm not ok. Everybody hates
> me.

>   AMY
> You didn't really send that email,
> did you?

>   SAM
> Of course I didn't! I would never
> send something that mean; I don't
> even think that stuff. Tiffany
> sent it and pretended it came from
> me. How could she do that?!

>   AMY
> I was just about to ask you: how
> DID she do that? How could Tiffany
> send an email from your address?

>   SAM
> (sigh) I gave her the password.
> WHEN she was my friend she asked me
> for it, like it was a friendship
> thing.

>   AMY
> No, no, no never never ...

>   SAM
>   (interrupting)
> I never talked to her boyfriend! I
> never said those hateful things
> that she said I said about the
> cheerleaders and I never sent that
> email!

>   AMY
> You can't give out your password,
> Sam. Not to her, not to anybody.

>   SAM
> Now the whole school hates me.

                    AMY
          Not everyone. I'm still here.

                    SAM
          Thanks.

                    AMY
          Come on. Let's go face the lynch
          mob.

                    SAM
          Are you serious?

                    AMY
          Yep. It'll just get worse the more
          time goes by.

Sam sighs, gets up.

                    SAM
          You're right. Of course. Don't
          you get sick of being right?

Amy smiles as they walk toward school...

                    AMY
          Hey, I have swim class with Tiffany
          tomorrow. You want me to
          waterboard her?

                    SAM
          It's tempting. Believe me.

The two friends go to face the skeptics.

                                        END

INT. RESTROOM AT SCHOOL NIGHT

NIKKI and SARA stand in front of a mirror. Nikki looks
at Sara's reflection, then...

                    NIKKI
        No, no, no. We're going to a
        party, not a yard sale.

                    SARA
        What!?

                    NIKKI
        Here, untuck this, pull your hair
        down a little, and use this.

                    SARA
        I don't wear lipstick.

                    NIKKI
        Obviously. Here.

She puts the lipstick on Sara.

                  NIKKI (CONT'D)
        There. Do you have any mascara?
        No, dumb question.

                    SARA
        I'm not trying to impress anyone,
        ok?

                    NIKKI
        You say that like it's a bad thing.
        There. You look hot.

                    SARA
        I do not. I'm smart but I'm not
        hot.

                    NIKKI
        Smart is the new sexy. Guys love
        smart girls; they figure you
        smolder underneath.

                    SARA
          (sarcastic)
        Yeah. I smolder.

                    NIKKI
          And smart with lipstick, hot
          tamale! That makes you hotter than
          90% of the girls out there.

Sara is surprised to hear herself called "hot" as Nikki
puts her finger on her like she's sizzling.

                    NIKKI (CONT'D)
          Tsssst! Oww! Burn it up! I feel
          smarter just by touching you.
          Let's go!

As they walk out.....

                    SARA
          Hey, rub a little of that
          confidence on me, will you?

                    NIKKI
          You won't need it. C'mon.

Sara straightens up her shoulders, takes a breath, and
walks out actually feeling attractive.

                                        END

TAMMY AND KATIE   *"MOM'S BOYFRIEND"*

INT. FOOD COURT DAY

KATIE is talking on her cell phone while TAMMY eats.

>   KATIE
>   (into phone)
>   Fine! Do what HE wants! Good-BYE!
>   (*she slams her phone shut*)
>   My mother makes me so mad
>   sometimes.
>
>   TAMMY
>   What's the problem?
>
>   KATIE
>   The PROBLEM is that she's dating
>   this ... guy. That's the problem.
>
>   TAMMY
>   She's dating someone? That's good,
>   isn't it?
>
>   KATIE
>   No, it isn't! He's not my dad, she
>   spends way too much time with him,
>   we don't need him around,
>   ....uggghhhhh! I wish he would
>   just go away.
>
>   TAMMY
>   Isn't he nice to your mom?
>
>   KATIE
>   Nice to her!? He treats her like
>   some queen. Makes me sick.
>
>   TAMMY
>   Is he nice to you and your brother?
>
>   KATIE
>   I don't care that he's nice. I
>   don't want him around.
>
>   TAMMY
>   So this is all about you, and too
>   bad what your mother wants, right?
>
>   KATIE
>   Why are you taking her side?

                    TAMMY
          I'm not. All I'm saying is, he
          doesn't sound like a guy who would
          slap your mother around, yell at
          you and your brother to stay out of
          his way, take money from her purse,
          get drunk and do it again ...
          making you wish you could protect
          your mother from all this misery
          but you can't so you just put up
          with it until your prayers are
          finally answered and he goes away
          for good.

Katie is dumbfounded.

                    TAMMY (CONT'D)
          It sounds a heckuva lot better than
          that to me.

                    KATIE
          Is that what happened to you?

                    TAMMY
          I'm not saying. I'm just saying if
          a guy treats you like a queen and
          makes your mother happy, what's
          your problem? It could be a whole
          lot worse.

She grabs her stuff and hurries away. Katie watches her
walk into the mall, then slowly, sheepishly, opens her
cell phone and calls.

                                        END

INT. LIBRARY DAY

AMBER is reading a book in the library when an excited
MEGAN slides in next to her.

                    MEGAN
               (trying to whisper)
          We got it! We're going!

                    AMBER
          Going where?

                    MEGAN
          We got in the dance competition!
          We're going to Chicago!

                    AMBER
          We're IN!?

They suddenly realize the librarian is glaring at them.
They bring the volume down, but not the excitement.

                    MEGAN
          It's in just five weeks so we have
          to work on all of our routines.
          Miss Bailey says we can use the
          upstairs gym, and me and you and
          Rachel and Kim are going to Chicago
          ...oh yeah .. going to Chicago.

                    AMBER
          Wow, dancing in Chicago. That
          means a hotel, and restaurants,
          we'll see the town...wait a minute.
          How much is this going to cost?

                    MEGAN
          Three hundred dollars each.

                    AMBER
          WHAT!?!

That was way too loud. They duck under the table, then
slowly peek back up to see if the librarian is looking.

                    AMBER (CONT'D)
          I can't afford $300. I can't go.

                    MEGAN
          You have to go. If you can't go we
          can't go.

                    AMBER
          I can't ask my mom for $300. She's
          working two jobs now. You three
          can go without me.

                    MEGAN
          Yeah, we could.   But we're not.

Pause. Megan thinks so hard you can smell the wood
burning.

                    MEGAN (CONT'D)
          Car wash. We'll wear the dance
          outfits and wash cars. If we don't
          get enough we'll do a yard sale,
          but you're going to Chicago.

                    AMBER
          You're the best.

Hug, fist-bump, arms over shoulders. Not whispering now…

                    BOTH
          We're going to Chicago, we're going
          to Chicago...

They dance their way out.

                                        END

COURTNEY & LILLY   *"TEN-DOLLAR TUNE"*

INT. SCHOOL   DAY

COURTNEY pulls LILLY off to the side…

                    COURTNEY
          Don't let him walk you home!   He's
          playing you like a ten-dollar
          violin.

                    LILLY
          Oh, good!   I love that kind of
          music. My mom plays the violin.

                    COURTNEY
          What? No, I mean … he's using you.
          He only wants you to walk with him
          to make Sophia jealous.

                    LILLY
          Why would she care? She takes the
          bus.

                    COURTNEY
          Ok, let me spell this out…

                    LILLY
          Ughh!   I *hate* spelling.

Ooo-kayy.   Courtney decides to explain it really clearly.

                    COURTNEY
          Lilly, he wants you to walk by the
          bus with him, so Sophia will see
          the two of you together, get
          jealous, and try to get HIM to like
          HER again. He's using you to get
          to her back.   Ok?

                    LILLY
          So I shouldn't walk home with him?

                    COURTNEY
          No.

                    LILLY
          Ok. But what about the violin?

                    COURTNEY
          Never mind! Wait here, I'll tell
          him myself.

As she walks off she mutters aloud…..

                    COURTNEY
      Oh, for the love of Pete …

                    LILLY
      Who's Pete?

                                                      END

"I love what I do. I take great pride in what I do. And
I can't do something halfway, three-quarters, nine-
tenths. If I'm going to do something, I go all the way."

                    - Tom Cruise

INT. MALL DAY

STACY and GWYNETH are walking; Gwyneth has a mysterious
grin on her face.

>   STACY
> There's a juice bar on this floor,
> wanna go?

>   GWYNETH
> Ok.

>   STACY
> What? Why do you have that look on
> your face?

>   GWYNETH
> What look?

>   STACY
> That look you always have when you
> have a good secret. Or when you're
> crazy about a guy. Or both. So
> who is he?

>   GWYNETH
> Excuse me Nancy Drew, but maybe I
> want to keep it a secret.

>   STACY
> Matthew? Brandon? That new guy
> Declan? C'maawwwnnnn. Someone is
> making my friend haaaappppy. Who?

>   GWYNETH
> I don't want to say. (Pause)
> Someone close to you.

>   STACY
> Close to me? Who is...waaait a
> minute, Jay and I have been going
> out a long time...

>   GWYNETH
>   (interrupting)
> I wouldn't ever go out with your
> boyfriend.

She starts to continue her train of thought, then stops.

>   STACY
> Why not? What's wrong with Jay?

                    GWYNETH
          Do you really want me to go down
          that road?

                    STACY
          No. So...."close to me". Who's
          close to me? hmmm

                    GWYNETH
          Ben.

                    STACY
          Ben? Who's Ben? The only Ben I
          know is my brother.

Gwyneth blushes.

                    STACY (CONT'D)
          What?! Yuck! Ben?!?! hahaha

                    GWYNETH
          Hey!

Stacy LAUGHS, then stops.

                    STACY
          Seriously, Gywn, you can't date my
          brother.

                    GWYNETH
          Why not?

                    STACY
          Because we're friends, it'll ruin
          everything. We'll end up keeping
          secrets from each other, and when
          you break up it'll be a mess.

                    GWYNETH
          No, it won't.

                    STACY
          Yes it will. You've already kept
          this from me. Don't date my
          brother.

                    GWYNETH
          Look at me, Stace. I like him. He
          likes me. You've had a guy for a
          long time. I finally found
          someone. Be my friend, ok?

They stare at each other for a moment.

                    STACY
          Ok.

They walk to the smoothie bar.

                    STACY (CONT'D)
          I saw him eat a worm once, you sure
          you want to kiss that mouth?

                    GWYNETH
          Knock it off.

                    STACY
          You want to know what else?

                    GWYNETH
          No!

                    STACY
          His left foot is bigger than his
          right.

                    GWYNETH
          Are either of them bigger than your
          mouth?

                    STACY
                (laughing)
          Ouch! Getting *nasty* in here.

                                        END

SCENE NOTES:

At the beginning of _"Cue The Actor"_ Hannah and Makenna are "in character"; have fun with the vocal change.

Amy sees the humor in the situation in _"Password Protection"_; at the end, they both can exercise their "gallows humor" expressions. When Samantha asks her if she's tired of always being right, it most likely comes out of true gratefulness.

In _"Mom's Boyfriend"_ Tammy can be played as having "been there/done that" or she could relive the entire ordeal. Is she also annoyed that her friend has it so good? Lots of conflict going on, meaning lots of ways to play her. Experiment.

For Megan and Amber (_"Dancin' Team"_) don't forget the environment -- they're in a library, most likely getting dirty looks from the librarian.

In _"You're Dating My What?!"_ Gwyneth and Stacy have fun together <u>even</u> when they're annoyed with each other.

TIFFANY & BRIANNA   *"RICH GIRLS"* (GETTING INTO CHARACTER)

INT. BACK OF SCHOOL AUDITORIUM   DAY

Two girls stand, looking at their classmates on the last day of school.

                    BRIANNA
          Look, Sarah "dressed up" in
          something she got at "Tar-jeay"

                    TIFFANY
          She looks like she's going to her
          'job' at the motel.

                    BRIANNA
          Speaking of 'lodging' (they laugh),
          are you going back to France this
          summer?

                    TIFFANY
          No way. We were supposed to, but I
          made such a fuss about it that
          Daddy is letting me go to Stockholm
          instead.

                    BRIANNA
          Stockholm! Good move, you go girl!

They "finger" high-five (so as not to ruin the manicure.)

                    BRIANNA (CONT'D)
          Is your brother going too?

                    TIFFANY
          No, Mr. Perfect is going to go to
          Africa with some group that teaches
          sports to those…. aborigines or
          whatever they are. Makes me gag.

                    BRIANNA
          He's probably the one who'll get
          sick. I heard they have all kinds
          of diseases over there.

                    TIFFANY
          I'll send him some Evian from the
          Ritz so that he doesn't have to
          drink the river water.

                    BRIANNA
          You're too kind.   Charity work
          becomes you.

                    TIFFANY
          Thank you, darling.

                    BRIANNA
          Maybe throw in a pillow mint, so
          his breath doesn't smell like snake
          meat.

As they leave….

                    TIFFANY
          Ick. Could you imagine?

                    BRIANNA
          No. Tell me about Stockholm. I
          heard you can really get into
          delicious trouble over there.

They laugh as they disappear.

                                              END

INT. LOBBY BY SCHOOL THEATRE   DAY

AVA and CHARISSE rush through the lobby to a list posted
on the wall.

              CHARISSE
     I have to get this part; my whole
     semester is planned around it.

              AVA
     There it is! The cast list is up!

As they look Ava's face brightens; Charisse is
disappointed.

              AVA (CONT'D)
     Alright! I'm playing Gwen. That's
     the part I wanted. It's small, but
     it's juicy. Where are you?

              CHARISSE
     No where. I didn't get Annabelle.
     Portia did. (*she turns away.*)
     I worked so hard on that ... it was
     a good audition. I sang my heart
     out.

              AVA
     I'm sorry. Portia is a good singer
     too though. (*on her look*) I'm
     just saying, it's not like you lost
     out to somebody who's no good, uh..

              CHARISSE
     You're not helping.

              AVA
     Sorry.

Charisse walks off as Ava turns back to read the cast
list.

              AVA (CONT'D)
     Charisse! Wait! You're on here;
     you're Merry Maid number 1.

Charisse comes back, looks at the list again.

              CHARISSE
     A Merry Maid!?

                    AVA
You and Sabrina are the Merry
Maids. Remember, they have a funny
song in Act 2 and they come back in
the end. You get to sing.

                    CHARISSE
Oh boy. Smallest part in the show.

                    AVA
Hey, you're IN the play. You go to
rehearsals, you go to the cast
parties... you're IN the show.

                    CHARISSE
Easy for you to say, you got the
part you wanted.

                    AVA
I didn't audition for the lead like
you did. My singing sounds like a
cat when you step on its tail. Besides, there are no small parts…

                    CHARISSE
Just small actors, yeah yeah.
(sigh) I should take it, shouldn't
I?

                    AVA
Uh, yeah! Besides, the lyrics are
funny.

                    CHARISSE
Yeah, they are. Me and Sabrina
could really have fun with it.

                    AVA
You'll be scene-stealers.

                    CHARISSE
Well, I wanted Annabelle, but...I
guess …

*As they walk away, Ava tries to cheer her up, SINGING an
old Rolling Stones' song.***

                    AVA
                (*singing*)
*"You can't always get what you
waa-annnt."*

                    CHARISSE
Good thing you didn't audition for
a singing part.

                    AVA
"You can't always get what you waa-
annt... ."

                    BOTH
"But if you try sometime, you just might
find .... YOU GET WHAT YOU NEEE-EEED!
Awwwww, babe!"

                                              END

** "You Can't Always Get What You Want". Jagger/Richard

From the Rolling Stones album "Let It Bleed". It's a good song. A
classic.

"Love yourself and everything else falls into line. You really do have to love yourself to get anything done in this world."

        - Lucille Ball

INT. FAST FOOD RESTAURANT DAY

SABRINA is talking on a cell phone with a sweet tone...

                    SABRINA
          (into phone)
     Sure, I'd be glad to...Friday at 6,
     I'll be there. Bye.
          (she hangs up)
     Ugghhh! I can't stand babysitting
     those kids!

                    KATE
     Then why are you doing it?

                    SABRINA
     Because I have NO money. When I
     get older I'm going to have lots of
     money and not have to do crummy
     jobs ever again.

                    KATE
     Have you got some big plan for
     making all this cash?

                    SABRINA
     If I don't make it as a famous
     singer, I'll marry it. I don't
     care. I'm sick of needing money.

                    KATE
     You'd marry a guy just because he's
     rich?

                    SABRINA
     Oh, like it's never been done
     before. Better than being broke.
     See that lady behind the counter?
     She's way old, she's like 40, and
     she's working <u>here</u>. Not me, babe.

                    KATE
     I'm making my own money. I'll
     probably go into medical something.
     Nurse, doctor, whatever. They make
     good money, and they help people.

                    SABRINA
     Singers help people. They can make
     you happy, help you after a break-
     up.

72

                    KATE
Yeah. But I can't think of
anything worse than being married
forever to a guy I can't stand.
Yeech. You can't sing your way out
of that. Tyler's parents are rich,
but would you want to be stuck with
HIM?

                    SABRINA
Eew. Okay, forget what I said
about marrying for money. I'm just
going to make my own and be
incredibly wealthy.

                    KATE
Me too. Girl power.

                    SABRINA
Girl power. (they eat) 'Course,
if you're a nurse you'll meet lots
of rich doctors. Who knows? You
might make it AND marry it.

                    KATE
Maybe. I know that someday I'd
like to have enough to be able to
help people like that old lady
handing out the fries.

They look at the lady sympathetically.

                    SABRINA
Yeah. I can hate my job for a
little while. But not forever.

They stop eating and watch the woman.

                                        END

                        73

EXT. PARKING LOT   DAY

EMILY and TRICIA lean against a car.

>   TRICIA
>   Ray wants me to do things with him,
>   you know, that I don't want to do.
>   Not that I don't want to, but ...
>   you know.
>
>   EMILY
>   So don't.
>
>   TRICIA
>   Easy for you to say. But he gets
>   all emotional and mad and I don't
>   want to lose him. Last night I
>   didn't want to go as far as he did,
>   and when we drove home he wouldn't
>   even speak to me.
>
>   EMILY
>   So, you didn't give in? Right?
>
>   TRICIA
>   No! Not really. Half.
>
>   EMILY
>   Half!? And he still wouldn't speak
>   to you? Trish, if he were "all
>   emotional" he'd talk to you, he'd
>   care how you feel. He's not "all
>   emotional", he only cares about one
>   emotion--- and it's way south of
>   the right side of that stupid brain
>   of his.
>
>   TRICIA
>   Stupid!? You wish you had someone
>   like Ray! Somebody who cared about
>   you but you don't, and I don't even
>   know why I'm talking to you about
>   it because you don't know what it's
>   like.

She storms off. Emily watches her leave, wishing she
could help her. Then her face brightens ever-so-subtly.
Tricia comes back, head down.

>   TRICIA (CONT'D)
>   I'm sorry, Em. Really. I'm sorry.

                    EMILY
        It's ok. First, though, you're
        wrong. I've been there.
        Second, I'm your friend. I respect
        you. You respect you. Find some
        guy that does too. It's not Ray.
        He doesn't respect you at all. You
        have to walk away.

She slowly nods her head 'yeah'.

                    EMILY (CONT'D)
        And you know what? In about two
        months we'll walk into the
        cafeteria and see some girl crying
        her eyes out because she gave him
        everything he wanted, and he still
        treated her like dirt and dumped
        her. And we'll both be glad it
        wasn't you. Two months, tops.

                    TRICIA
        How did you do it when you went
        through this?

                    EMILY
        Tell you all about it on the way
        home. Let's go.

They walk off.

                                                    END

"Courage is being scared to death, but saddling up anyway."

— John Wayne

CHAPTER THREE

Boy / Boy Scenes

INT. SCHOOL DANCE HALL NIGHT

BRETT and ETHAN stand off to the side surveying the dancers as the music plays...

> BRETT
> What do you think? Should we get out there and dance?
> (on his look)
> Not with each other, wise-guy. Are you gonna ask somebody?

> ETHAN
> I don't know. Maybe Megan. She sits next to me in class sometimes. She's looking this way! Don't look.

> BRETT
> DON'T look? Why not? This is the time TO look. Look at her. Right now, look at her and smile.

Ethan does, and his smile slowly widens.

> ETHAN
> I think I'm going to go talk to her.

> BRETT
> Go to it, man. Confidence. She'll love a confident guy.

> ETHAN
> How do you know?

> BRETT
> I'm an expert, I have two sisters. Confidence.

> ETHAN
> Confidence.

Ethan starts to walk toward her, then Brett pulls him back.

> BRETT
> Hey, E....as long as you're going, could you ask her if Laura likes me? No, don't. Yeah, do. Ok?

> ETHAN
> Just come with me, Expert.

78

Ethan grabs him by the sleeve and drags him with him.

> BRETT
> Wait, what if she doesn't like me,
> what if......?

> ETHAN
> Where's that confidence now, huh?
> Talk the talk, walk the walk.
> C'mon.

Brett breathes deep, and they march into that mysterious
valley where dreams live and die.

END

TROY & CHAD   *"THE PARENT TRAP"*

INT. LOCKER ROOM DAY

TROY and CHAD finish dressing after practice.

                    TROY
          I'm whipped. I'm gonna flop in
          front of the tv and lay around like
          a big old dog tonight.

                    CHAD
          Me too. Just rest up for
          tomorrow's game.

                    TROY
          Did you say your dad was coming?

                    CHAD
          Yeah.   That's what he said,
          anyway. We'll see. I figure he
          and my mother can sit on opposite
          sides of the gym.

                    TROY
          Good thing it's a big gym. Do they
          get along any better now?

                    CHAD
          Nah. Same as always.
             (pause)
          I like my dad, and I like my mom.
          I just don't like 'em together.
          Always a fight.

                    TROY
          That's just who they are; doesn't
          have a thing to do with you.

                    CHAD
          I know. I keep telling that to my
          little sister, that it doesn't mean
          we were bad kids or anything. It's
          them, not us. I think she's
          finally getting it. She just...
          wishes, you know?

                    TROY
          You're a good big brother, man.

                    CHAD
             (softly)
          I'm tryin'.

They continue getting dressed to go outside.

                    CHAD (Cont'd)
          Your parents coming tomorrow?

                    TROY
          Yeah, they wouldn't miss it.
          You'll hear 'em, believe me.

                    CHAD
          That's cool. Your parents are ok.

                    TROY
          Yeah, they are. Thanks.

A moment of silence as they finish stuffing their gym
bags, thinking about their very different situations at
home.

                    TROY (CONT'D)
          What are you doing after the game?

                    CHAD
          I don't know, that'll be another
          fight, no matter which one I go
          with. Maybe I can get a referee to
          work a little overtime up in the
          parent section.

                    TROY
          Maybe. He'd be calling a lot of
          personal fouls.

                    CHAD
          Oh yeah.

Small smiles. Troy throws his bag over his shoulder.

                    TROY
          Hey, good luck.   See you tomorrow.

They head out, one exits downstage left, the other
downstage right. Different directions, to very
different homes.

                                        END

INT. INDUSTRIAL TECH CLASS DAY

ZACH is texting with his phone when NICK walks up wearing goggles and holding a drill.

                    NICK
          What'cha doing?

                    ZACH
          Sending a note to Lana.

                    NICK
          I thought you weren't going to be
          seeing her anymore.

                    ZACH
          I'm not.

                    NICK
          So, you broke up with her?

                    ZACH
          Almost.

                    NICK
          Almost?

                    ZACH
          Almost done.

                    NICK
          Hold it!

Nick flips his goggles up and holds the drill like a gun.

                    NICK (CONT'D)
          You are NOT texting a break-up.

He grabs the phone out of Zach's hand, reads it, hits 'delete'.

                    ZACH
          What are you doing?! We used to text
          all the time, she won't care how I do
          it. It's technology.

                    NICK
          It's rude. R-U-D, OMG. Man up.
          Go find her and tell her to her
          face.

                    ZACH
          No, I don't need to. I can't.

                    NICK
          Why not?

                    ZACH
          Because ... you know, she might
          cry, it gets messy. She'll be
          fine with this.

                    NICK
          Not buying it. Look, me and you
          are friends. I'm doing you a
          favor.
               (*takes battery out of phone*)
          I'm protecting you from every other
          girl in this school.

Zach sighs, knows he's right but really doesn't want to
face her.

                    ZACH
          Man, ...I was almost done.

                    NICK
          You sure were. Go talk to her.

He shuffles off. Turns back to plead his case again,
sees Nick's determined face and drill in his hand, turns
back around and walks.

                    NICK (CONT'D)
          You'll thank me later.

                    ZACH
          'Thanks' probably won't be the word
          I use.

Nick puts the battery in his pocket, goggles back down,
and gets back to work.

                                              END

MITCH & MICHAEL *"IT TAKES A THIEF"*

INT. LOCKER HALLWAY DAY

MICHAEL is putting his books in his locker when MITCH approaches him and whispers.

MITCH
Hey, bud, need your help. I need some money…

MICHAEL
Dude, I am stone broke.

MITCH
I know, that's what I want to talk to you about. You know those cameras they just got in the tech lab? I looked 'em up, they cost about 3 grand apiece. I know a guy who'll get me 800 bucks for each one I get him.

MICHAEL
Hold it. What?

MITCH
I got a plan to take 'em. I can jimmy the upper window open during lab, then go in at night and flip 'em out. In and out in ten minutes.

MICHAEL
Mitch, I uh....I don't ...whew, I wish somehow we never had this conversation. Don't tell me any more, and I won't say a word.

MITCH
Heck no you won't say a word, 'cause you'll be with me. I need somebody to load the trunk and drive the car.

MICHAEL
No, I can't.

MITCH
Yes you can, I told you about this because we're friends. I need you. Are we friends or not?

MICHAEL
Yeah, but,… I'm not a thief...

                    MITCH
          It's not stealing, they got
          insurance. And we both need the
          money. C'mon. We're buds.

He puts his arm on Michael's shoulder as they walk.

                    MICHAEL
          I don't know why I let you do this
          to me...

                    MITCH
          Because you're smart. And you're
          gonna be rich.

                    MICHAEL
          You know what, hold it. I can't.
          I'm not a thief, and I can't do it.

He stops. Mitch takes his arm off Michael's shoulder.
Stand-off.

                    MITCH
          I thought we were friends.

                    MICHAEL
          That's up to you. I'm not going.
          And you shouldn't either.

Mitch stares at him a moment. Is that a threat? Will
Michael tell on him? Mitch looks down at the floor.

Is he feeling guilty? Reconsidering? No.

                    MITCH
          Rocco. He'll do it, he needs the
          cash, and he owes me. I gotta go.
          You're missing out, bud. Hey, not
          a word, you promised.

Mitch smiles as he walks away, turns and puts his finger
to his lips as in "Shhh", leaving Michael in a huge moral
dilemma.

                                        END

"MY LITTLE BROTHER, NOT YOURS"

INT. CAFETERIA DAY

TY and WYATT open their bags of lunch.

> WYATT
> Oh, man! I got my little brother's
> lunch! Jelly on raisin bread,
> yuck. He is so lame.

> TY
> Yeah, he is a nerd-brain.

Wyatt stops, puts down the sandwich.

> WYATT
> What?!

> TY
> What?

> WYATT
> What did you say? Don't you ever
> talk about my brother like that.

> TY
> Well, you just said...I was just
> agreeing with you...

> WYATT
> Don't be bad-mouthing my brother
> just because of the way he eats.

> TY
> I wasn't. You were.

> WYATT
> Well, I can talk about him like
> that, you can't. Alright? He's my
> brother, not yours.

> TY
> Alright, I won't talk about your
> brother.
>   (pause)
> Except to say... he takes after
> you. And you....are a grade-A
> whack-o.

He flicks a corn chip at him; they look at each other
like they're about to fight, then BUST UP LAUGHING.
(They *could start a food fight here if the room allows,
or just improv an insult-a-thon.*)

"Comedy is acting out optimism."

         - Robin Williams

INT. CLASSROOM DAY

DAVID and BRANDON are about to take a history test.
David hasn't studied.

>   DAVID
> Psst. Brandon! Do you know this
> stuff?

>   BRANDON
> Most of it. I worked on it all
> night.

>   DAVID
> Great. I need the answers.

>   BRANDON
> What? No, I can't do that.

>   DAVID
> Just write some down and pass 'em
> to me. Make some of 'em wrong if
> you want. I just need a "C".
> C'mon. I need it.

>   BRANDON
> I can't. I've got a 3.9. I can't
> lose it.

>   DAVID
> You won't, I promise. Come on.

David nods to the floor.   Brandon stares at him for a
moment, then checks the teacher. He sighs, starts
writing a few answers on a scrap of paper. He drops the
paper on the floor.

David drops his pen, reaches down and picks up the pen
and the answers. He starts to copy them. Brandon buries
his head in his test, writing furiously.

>   TEACHER (O.S.)
> David. Brandon. Pens down.

They look up, startled. Both boys slowly drop their
pens.

>   TEACHER O.S. (CONT'D)
> Now, take your test papers and tear
> them in half. Your cheating has
> earned you an "F".

                    BRANDON
        What?! No! We didn't, we just ...

He stops. He can't lie about it, but his frustration is
boiling over.

                    BRANDON (CONT'D)
        I'VE NEVER HAD AN F in my life!

                    TEACHER (O.S.)
        And now you have. Intelligence
        without moral character is failure.
        You both have shown your character
        today, and you've failed. F.

Brandon is mortified; he buries his head in his hands in
anguish.

                    DAVID
        Dude, sorry. I owe you.

If looks could kill. Brandon stares at him for a moment,
wanting to strangle him, then crumples the torn pages of
his test.

                                            END

*"With any part you play, there is a certain amount of
yourself in it. There has to be, otherwise it's not
acting. It's lying."*

                    - Johnny Depp

EXT. FRONT PORCH   DAY

ANDREW is looking at a magazine when NATHAN walks up.

                    NATHAN
          What're you doing?

                    ANDREW
          Looking at new cars. I'm looking
          for the one I'm gonna buy when I
          get a license.

                    NATHAN
          Uh, little early, isn't it? Those
          cars won't be new by the time you
          get to drive.

                    ANDREW
          Exactly. And with any luck by then
          I'll be able to afford it. What do
          you think of this one?

                    NATHAN
          Cool, but how are you going to get
          money for this? You think your dad
          is going to buy it for you?

                    ANDREW
          Yeah, right. Mr. "Money Doesn't
          Grow On Trees" is still stuck in
          the 80's.

                    NATHAN
          Same here. Our car still has
          window cranks. So where are you
          getting the money for one of these?

                    ANDREW
          My new business. I hire myself out
          to old-school parents like ours,
          and I install their kid's game
          software and show 'em how to use
          it.

                    NATHAN
          Really? You think parents are gonna
          hire you for that?

                    ANDREW
          I just started yesterday and I have two
          customers lined up already. Thirty
          bucks a piece. Look at this
          convertible; what do you think?

NATHAN
Thirty bucks a piece? Times two, times
5 days, times...whoa! Hey, do you need
any help in this business?

ANDREW
If it starts booming I can hire you.
You want to be my assistant?

NATHAN
Yeah! Deal. (they shake on it) And
yeah, that looks cool. Girls like
convertibles.

ANDREW
That's what I figure too. All we
have to do is find this exact car
in a few years.

NATHAN
Heck, by then we'll be able to just
think of it and Google will find it.
Hey! look at this retro: a '57 T-Bird

ANDREW
Sweet.

END

*"Celebrity … that's the worst thing that can happen to
an actor."*

- John Cusack

EXT.   ABANDONED HOUSE   NIGHT

Two guys sneak up through the high grass and brush to a
window of an old house.   They speak in hushed tones.

                    NICHOLAS
          This'll be the find of the century.
          We could hang out in this house and
          no one would ever find us.

                    RYAN
          It looks like it was built a
          hundred years ago. I bet nobody's
          lived here in at least 5 years.

                    NICHOLAS
          There's the window. C'mon. This
          is going to be so cool.

Ryan and Nicholas hide under the ledge, check the
surroundings, then reach up and LOOK through the window.
At first they can't see very much.

                    RYAN
          We might have to clean it up a
          little, but…. Ahhhh!

Their eyes widen in shock. Ryan covers his mouth to
prevent any more noise. He and Nicholas GASP, then DUCK!

                    RYAN (CONT'D)
                (loud whisper)
          Did you see that?

                    NICHOLAS
                (whispers)
          Shh. Ok. We gotta make sure.
          Let's look again. If he sees us,
          you run that way. We'll meet back
          at my house.

He nods to the window. They slowly reach back up and
peek through. Their eyes get big, mouths open.

Nicholas ducks back down; Ryan is frozen. Nicholas pulls
him down.

                    RYAN
          We gotta do something.

                    NICHOLAS
          Yeah.   We're calling the cops.

                         92

                    RYAN

        What if they don't believe us?

                  NICHOLAS

        They will. Come on!

They race off with frightened/determined looks.

                                        END

INT. ART CLASS DAY

PAYTON and CHRIS are painting Thanksgiving scenes.

> CHRIS
> What's your family doing for
> Thanksgiving this year?

> PAYTON
> Pretty much the same thing we do
> every year.

> CHRIS
> A tradition? Cool. What do you
> do?

> PAYTON
> My mother puts a turkey in the
> oven, then we all go hike up this
> hill that overlooks the entire
> city, and we think about what we're
> thankful for. Stuff like that.
> Then we come back, eat 'til we're
> stuffed, and argue football with
> our uncles and cousins. Same thing
> every year.

> CHRIS
> Your family argues too?

> PAYTON
> Oh yeah. Loud.
> (imitating his uncle)
> *"Emmitt Smith?!??! We can talk
> football ONLY if you understand
> that Walter Payton is the greatest
> running back who evah lived! If
> you don't know that, you don't know
> football!"*

> CHRIS
> Same thing here, only in our
> 'tradition' it's politics.
> (*imitates her father*)
> *"Oh, you're an expert alright.
> THIS brilliant analysis from
> someone who voted for George W.
> C-Student! **Twice**!"*

> PAYTON
> Loud and proud. And that's **before**
> they pull out the wine.

They laugh.

                         CHRIS
          Don't you wish you could just go
          somewhere else for Thanksgiving and
          avoid your family?

He pauses, thinks about it.

                         PAYTON
          No. No, I kind of like it the way
          it is.

Chris considers this sentiment as they go back to work on
their art pieces.

                                                    END

"Having a family is like having a bowling alley installed
in your brain."

                    - Martin Mull

INT. SCHOOL HALLWAY DAY

An athlete, AUSTIN, walks past a classroom and sees a smaller frightened boy (STEWART) peeking out of the doorway.

Stewart ducks back in, then peeks out again.

>   AUSTIN
>   Hey. You ok?

>   STEWART
>   ....yeah.

>   AUSTIN
>   Ok.

He starts to leave, turns back.

>   AUSTIN (CONT'D)
>   Nothing's wrong?

>   STEWART
>   Some guys are waiting for me.
>   They're going to pull my underwear
>   over my head and throw me into the
>   girl's restroom.

>   AUSTIN
>   Why?

>   STEWART
>   I bumped one of them when I sat
>   down.

>   AUSTIN
>   That's it? Doesn't sound like a
>   crime to me. I'm Austin.

>   STEWART
>   I know. Stewart.

>   AUSTIN
>   These guys aren't my team-mates,
>   are they?

>   STEWART
>   No, just some mean guys.

>   AUSTIN
>   What are you going to do?

                    STEWART
          Wait here 'til the bell rings I
          guess.

                    AUSTIN
          That'll get you a detention.
          C'mon. Walk with me. You won't
          get hurt.

                    STEWART
          Really!? (*then, suspicious*) Wait.
          You won't throw me into them, will
          you?

At first Austin is offended by the question, but sees the
fear in Stewart's face.

                    AUSTIN
          No. Don't be afraid of me. And I
          won't be afraid of them. We'll
          walk right through 'em. C'mon
          ...Stewart?

Stewart nods "yes" as they walk together.

                    AUSTIN (CONT'D)
          Stewart, when you see the guys,
          laugh out loud like I just said
          something funny, got it?

                    STEWART
          Got it. Thanks.   …
          You're lucky.

                    AUSTIN
          I guess I am.

They walk tall.

                                             END

IAN, ANTHONY, TED & NICK   *"HAMLET FOR TOUGH GUYS"*

INT. REHEARSEL HALL   DAY

Two boys, IAN and ANTHONY, are rehearsing for a play.

> IAN
> *"Have you had quiet guard?"*

> ANTHONY
> *"Not a mouse stirring".*

> IAN
> *"Well, good night. If you meet Horatio and Marcellus, bid them make haste."*

> ANTHONY
> *"I think I hear them. Stand, ho! Who's there?"*

Two tough-guy classmates, NICK and TED, enter and interrupt.

> TED
> <u>We're</u> here, wussy-boys.

> NICK
> What'cha doing? "Play practice" for your little ***theatre*** play.

> IAN
> We're rehearsing.

> ANTHONY
> It's called Hamlet. You've heard of Shakespeare, right?

> TED
> Ooooh, Shakespeare!

> NICK
> Forsooth!   (He does a pirouette).

Anthony figures that if he wants to stay out of the dumpster he'd better outwit them.

> ANTHONY
> Mel Gibson from all the Lethal Weapon movies played Hamlet. So did Marlon Brando, the Godfather and the Wild One, where he played the head of a motorcycle gang. You like Vin Diesel? Jason Statham?

98

                    NICK
          Uh, yeah.

Ian turns away.

                    ANTHONY
          Got their start in high school
          plays, just like this one.
          Besides, that's where all the girls
          are.

                    TED
          Yeah, right, you guys are gonna get
          all the girls.

                    NICK
          C'mon, let's let the wusseys go
          back to their "play practice".

The tough guys exit, stage left.

                    IAN
          Marlon Brando played Hamlet? Vin
          Diesel did high school plays?

                    ANTHONY
          Maybe. I don't know.

                    IAN
          You don't know!?! Whoa, you made
          that up? You lied to those guys?

                    ANTHONY
          I didn't lie, I ... improvised.

They high-five each other with big smiles.

                    IAN
          That's improvising all right. You
          get a Tony AND an Oscar.

                    ANTHONY
          Thank you, my liege.

                    IAN
          Whew. I need some water. Vin
          Diesel playing Hamlet, that's
          great.... .

They exit stage right.

                                        END

Scene Notes:

One way to play Chad in *"The Parent Trap"* is to add the subtext that his parents were divorced a long time ago, and that his situation is nothing new to him. He's free to search for the dry humor in his parents' actions, because he knows it's not going to change. Does he envy Troy's family life, or does he just want to let Troy know how good he has it?

In *"Text The News"* the industrial tech class can be changed to fit the props at hand.

In *"It Takes A Thief"* though Mitch takes his pause at the end (when he's told that Michael won't go with him), he doesn't give away whether he's reconsidering on moral grounds, or thinking of another way to carry out the plan. Hopefully, it will surprise us.

Everyone knows a 'David' (*"'F' in Integrity"*), the guy who *"just needs a few of the answers"*. How do you play him so that he's not a cliché'? Doesn't he really believe that it'll be ok? That this will be the last time? At the end, is Brandon more angry at David, or at himself?

What did Nicholas and Ryan see when they looked through the window in *"This Old House"*? Stolen property? A thief? Both? A gang? See something; visualize it.

In *"Thanksgiving Wishes"* have fun imitating your family members … use an accent, slur your words, use gestures. Big and bold impersonations will be a nice departure from the rest of the scene.

Scene Notes

In _"Bully For You"_ does Stewart's posture and walk change a little at the end? How do you think our athlete Austin will react when he sees the guys that have been terrorizing Stewart?

"Hamlet for Tough Guys" is a fun, pretty self-explanatory scene; the actors just need to pay attention to their staging. Nick needs space for the pirouette; when Ian has to turn away (presumably to laugh at their choices of 'fine' actors) he needs to let the audience see his aside. Same with Anthony when he figures out a way to stay out of the dumpster. Let the audience (or the camera) see your expression, and let it be in your body, too.

"It would be wonderful to enjoy success, without seeing envy in the eyes of those around you."

- Marilyn Monroe

101

"Acting is not being emotional, but being able to express
emotion."

- Kate Reid

CHAPTER FOUR

Single Actor / Off-Screen Actor

INT. LIVING ROOM NIGHT

A very sheepish and apologetic JESSE is standing in front
of his father.

                    JESSE
          Dad...it just happened. I didn't
          think his shirt would rip, we were
          just goofing around.

                    FATHER (O.S.)
          You were goofing around **in class**?
          Where was the teacher?

                    JESSE
          She went down to the principal's
          office to get an aspirin.

                    FATHER (O.S.)
          I'm not surprised. So you just
          grabbed at Andre and his shirt
          ripped. Was he embarrassed?

                    JESSE
          Yeah. He got laughed at a little.

                    FATHER (O.S.)
          Did you laugh at him?

                    JESSE
          No. And I said I was sorry.

                    FATHER (O.S.)
          Good. At least you did that. But
          we both know that 'sorry' isn't
          good enough.

                    JESSE
          What do you mean?

                    FATHER (O.S.)
          You ripped his shirt. You have to
          pay for it.

                    JESSE
          Pay for it? How am I gonna...?

                    FATHER (O.S.)
          You'll use the money you got for
          your birthday.

                              JESSE
          Dad! I was going to use that money
          for a new XR-7!

                         FATHER (O.S.)
          If he had ruined something of yours
          you'd expect him to replace it,
          wouldn't you? Pay him tomorrow.

As disappointed as he is, Jesse knows he's right.

                              JESSE
               Yes sir.

                         FATHER (O.S.)
          And hey, Jesse. I know you didn't
          mean it, and I'm glad you said you
          were sorry. We've all goofed off.
          But sometimes ….we have to pay for
          it. You understand?

                              JESSE
               Yeah.

Jesse goes to get the money.

                                             END

ZOE (on phone)**/ BROTHER** (V.O.)   *"GOTCHA BACK"*

INT. MALL   DAY

ZOE is walking and talking to Sabrina on her cell in the mall.

>   ZOE
>   O-M-G you wouldn't believe what I
>   found! The cutest lip gloss in
>   Triple Shine Pink. Trevor loves
>   it, he told me so. …..I'm at the
>   mall. You are too?! LOL! I'll
>   find you!

As she sits on a bench in the middle of the stores, she gets a beep and looks at her phone.

>   ZOE (CONT'D)
>   Ugh! Hold on.   It's my brother.
>   *(clicks phone)*
>   What, Philip?

>   PHILIP (V.O.)
>   Can you hang out there for a few
>   more hours? My, uh, 'friend' is
>   going to stay a little longer.

>   ZOE
>   A few HOURS!? No. I have dance
>   class at six!

>   PHILIP (V.O.)
>   Well, you'll have to get a ride, or
>   …skip the class. See a movie.

>   ZOE
>   I can't! You stole half my money!

>   PHILIP (V.O.)
>   I needed it.   Look, I don't know
>   what you're going to do, but do
>   something, and don't show up until
>   after 7.

Her expression turns from disgust to a mischievous grin with a glint in her eye…

>   ZOE
>   Hey, Philip, you know what? I just
>   ran into Lauren here at the mall
>   and told her you were home and that
>   she should drop by and see you.
>   Won't that be nice?

She smiles as he rants.

                    ZOE (cont'd)
          Oh, that's right, you're with
          Amber. I'm sorry, my bad. Well,
          the three of you have a good time!
               (clicks him off)
          That'll teach him to keep his word.
               (clicks over to
               Sabrina)
          Sabrina? Meet you at Lulu's.

She closes the phone with a sly grin.

                                        END

[Note: This scene could easily be played out with an on-stage actor playing Philip (on camera it could be split-screen).]

INT. CLASSROOM DAY

TY looks at his shoes as the room clears out. Finally
it's just him and his Teacher.

                    TYLER
     What did you want to see me about?

                    TEACHER (O.S.)
     I saw you and Sara in the hall,
     heard what you were saying ...

                    TYLER
     So?

                    TEACHER (O.S.)
     Let me finish.   It just seemed
     that you were treating her very
     badly. Your comments were
     insulting to her.

                    TYLER
     What?! She's my girlfriend, she
     knows what I mean. That isn't
     anybody else's business.

                    TEACHER (O.S.)
     No, this isn't official business.
     But every woman, no matter how old,
     deserves respect. Do you respect
     Sara?

                    TYLER
     I just said, she's my girlfriend.
     There's a lot of other girls out
     there, and I picked her. Alright?

                    TEACHER (O.S.)
     You didn't answer my question.

                    TYLER
     And I'm not going to. I'll talk to
     her any way I want. If she ain't
     with it, there's the door, she can
     leave. But she hasn't, has she?
     She'd rather have a man than a
     wuss.

                    TEACHER (O.S.)
          So insulting her makes you feel
          like a man? That's not manhood,
          Ty; that's being a jerk.

                    TYlER
          Look, you said this wasn't
          official, so I'm out of here.

As he walks out...

                    TEACHER (O.S.)
          Ty? If she has any self-respect,
          she will find that door and walk
          out.

                    TYLER
          That ain't gonna happen. And you
          just stay away from her, you got
          me?

                    TEACHER (O.S.)
          Are you threatening me?

Tyler is about to, thinks better of it. He leaves in a
huff.

                                              END

KYLE & DAD   *"YOU SHOULD'VE SEEN IT"*

INT. LIVING ROOM   NIGHT

KYLE is describing the game to his often-absent dad, who is reading a newspaper…

> KYLE
> You should've seen it!   I was coming down the right side, Brandon kicked the ball on kind of a curve, like Beckham used to do, and I ran right into it and WHAM!   Headed it right into the goal. It was great! Greatest day I've ever had.

> DAD (O.S.)
> Even better than that time I took you fishing?

> KYLE
> Uh, yeah…. when I was 9, that was good. But this game was really awesome! The whole team mobbed me. It was the only goal of the game and they carried me off the field on their shoulders! I wish you could've been there, Dad.

No reaction from Dad, who continues reading.

> KYLE (CONT'D)
> You might have been proud.

Kyle leaves.

END

Scene Notes:

In _"Do The Right Thing"_ Jesse has to do a lot of listening.   His face will show us what he's feeling when his dad is talking to him.

Zoe (_"Gotcha Back"_) has a cleverness, and an ability to switch tracks in mid-sentence. Her eyes and expressions, with her vocal changes, will show us her change from fun-loving to wicked and then back to fun-loving.

No matter what we may think of Tyler's attitude ("R-E-S-P-E-C-T"), HE thinks there is nothing wrong with being the boss and treating his girl like his slave. Do you think he grew up witnessing that in his own home? Find his truth.

Kyle has to try his best (twice) to get his dad to congratulate him in _"You Should've Seen It"_. Kyle fails, but he doesn't know that until the very end.

INT. LIVING ROOM   EVENING

A young girl, SOPHIA, waves good-bye to Mom and her date
as they exit the doorway and the babysitter, ALLISON
steps in.

                    SOPHIA
                (enthusiastic)
          Bye Mom! I'll miss you.
                (flat, icy)
          Hello Allison.

                    ALLISON
          Thrilled to see you too, Sophia.

She slams the door and dashes all hopes of a good
evening.

                    SOPHIA
          I want some ice cream.

Allison picks up the Mom's note.

                    ALLISON
          It says right here that you just
          had some.

                    SOPHIA
          I want some more!

                    ALLISON
          Here's a word you may not be
          familiar with: "No!"

Sophia sticks out her tongue at Allison.

                    ALLISON (CONT'D)
          Do that again and I'll put pepper
          on it.

Sophia crosses her arms and pouts.

                    SOPHIA
          I don't like you.

                    ALLISON
                (dry, sarcastic)
          Oh no. I'm crushed.

Sophia instinctively sticks out her tongue again.

                    ALLISON (CONT'D)
         Ok, now where's that pepper?

Sophia's eyes widen: *'She might do it.'*

Allison looks at her both confident and satisfied.

                                              END

"Love the art in yourself, not yourself in the art."

                          - Konstantin Stanislavsky

INT. LIVING ROOM NIGHT

DARA is both reading a magazine and listening to music
through her headphones, bobbing her head with a
mischievous smile, as though she's listening to salty
lyrics.

Her mother bursts through the door and yells.

                MOTHER (O.S.)
      Get your shoes on, we have to go!

                DARA
      What? I don't wanna go anywhere.

                MOTHER (O.S.)
      Get dressed! We have to go get
      Jeremy.

                DARA
      Let the little twerp walk home for
      once. Why does he always get a
      chauffeur?

                MOTHER (O.S.)
      Jeremy's been in a car accident,
      he's at the hospital. Now get
      going!

A door slams. Dara looks in disbelief (and more
than a little guilt).

                DARA
      What? I ... I'm coming, I'm
      sorry...

She pops off the headphones, then gets up and out.

                              END

"Actors ought to be larger than life. You come across
quite enough ordinary, nondescript people in daily life;
I don't see why you should be subjected to them on the
stage too."

- Ninon de Lenclos

INT. LOBBY OUTSIDE OF ARENA   DAY

EMMA is taping her rant about Clint, the boy who dumped her, so she can put it on YouTube.

> EMMA
> (into camera)
> Are you rolling? Ok. My name is
> Emma, and this spot right behind me
> is the exact location where Clint
> Donovan dumped me. Right here at
> this basketball arena. Yes, Clint
> Donovan, big-time basketball
> player, all the fans love him, blah
> blah blah. He's a cheat, and a
> liar...you wouldn't believe the
> things he said to me when we were
> alone "oh I'm crazy about you, I
> want you to be my girl mmm mmm mmm"
> and he was saying the **same thing** to
> Amy. Amy Finich. So the next time
> you see this big-time athlete and
> start to cheer for him, just
> remember that inside, where it
> counts, he is empty, and I will
> never EVER give him even the
> slightest...

She stops suddenly, looks away from the camera. There is someone looking at her, maybe smiling at her. It might be Clint. She pauses, embarrassed, gives the cameraman a CUT signal...

> EMMA (CONT'D)
> Cut for a second.

She then gives a small smile, then bigger, maybe a subtle finger-wave...then looks back at the camera.

> EMMA (CONT'D)
> (to cameraman)
> Can you erase that? (on his look)
> Don't judge me!

She walks off in the direction of the distraction.

                                        END

Scene Notes:

Though the actor playing Allison in _"Babysitting.."_ may be working with a fellow actor or an instructor, in her mind she needs to see a 6 year old brat.

In _"Accident"_ Dara has a choice either to make a quick emotional change -- immediate in both expression and body language -- or a slow realization. Does she jump up? Does she have trouble believing what she just heard? Does she love her brother?

We all know an Emma (_"YouTube Rant"_); you don't have to complicate it.   It can and should be fun.

INT. PRINCIPAL'S OFFICE   DAY

DEREK walks in with a curious smile.

> DEREK
> You wanted to see me about an award
> of some kind?

> SOCIAL WORKER (O.S.)
> No, I'm sorry about that, that's
> not why we called you in here.

> DEREK
> Then what is it?

> SOCIAL WORKER (O.S.)
> We just got a phone call from the
> police. Your brother is in their
> custody.

His face sinks, but he's not shocked.

> DEREK
> Should've known. Same thing?

He gets an affirmative nod, then...

> SOCIAL WORKER (O.S.)
> Do you know where your parents
> might be?

> DEREK
> No idea. I'll go down there.
> (*He starts to go, pauses*)
> Don't tell my little sister about
> this, ok?

> SOCIAL WORKER (O.S.)
> Of course. He's at the Oak Street
> Station.

> DEREK
> I know the way.

He exits.

                                        END

Scene Note:

The previous scene and the next scene set in the Principal's office are variations on the same theme ... a family member has let them both down.

Their reactions -- one of dutiful resignation, one of denial/sadness -- come from their back-stories. What kind of a childhood do you think Derek and Mickey had?

MICKEY / SOCIAL WORKER O.S.)   *"VARIATION ON A THEME"*

INT. PRINCIPAL'S OFFICE DAY

MICKEY, whose mother is a drug addict and father is an
absent rock-and-roll guitarist, shuffles into the office
and plops down in front of a social worker.

                    MICKEY
          Why did you pull me out of class?
          What did I do?

                    MAN IN SUIT (O.S.)
          Nothing, you're fine, but...your
          mother has been arrested. She's
          been remanded to a state hospital.

                    MICKEY
          What?! A state hospital where?
          When? I want to go see her.

                    MAN IN SUIT (O.S.)
          I'm sorry. She was taken away
          this morning. You will be in the
          care of your grandmother; she's
          flying in tonight.

                    MICKEY
          No! I don't even know my
          grandmother. I haven't seen her
          since I was like ...two. I want to
          be with my father.

                    MAN IN SUIT (O.S.)
          Your father is unavailable....

                    MICKEY
            (interrupts)
          Just call him! He'll come and get
          me. You didn't even call him!

                    MAN IN SUIT (O.S.)
          Your father was contacted this
          morning in New York. He declined
          to come back. I'm sorry.

Mickey's head begins to sink as the shock sets in.

                    MICKEY
          He said 'no'? He's not coming
          back for me?

She hangs her head as the tears begin to fall.

                                        END

"*Dream as if you'll live forever, live as if you'll die tomorrow.*"

— James Dean

INT. KITCHEN DAY

Mom is in the kitchen when LAUREN rushes in...

                    LAUREN
          Mom, I NEED some money for tonight.
          Everybody is going to the Crab
          Shack after the game and I can't go
          with no money.

                    MOM (O.S.)
          Did you ask your father?

                    LAUREN
          Yes, and he said I have to earn it
          but I can't! I don't have time to
          work for it and he won't just give
          it to me.

                    MOM (O.S.)
          No, we earn our money around here.

                    LAUREN
          He gives YOU money, and you don't
          work.

                    MOM (O.S.)
          EXCUSE me? You want to explain
          that comment while I'm cooking or
          doing the laundry?

                    LAUREN
          Ok, that's not what I meant. I
          meant you don't GO to work.
             (Mom glares)
          I mean. ... you know what I mean.
          This isn't going the way I wanted.

                    MOM (O.S.)
          I'll bet it isn't. Tell you what:
          I'll loan you the money if you can
          name ten things I do for this
          family.

                    LAUREN
          That's easy, laundry, like you
          said, dinner, chauffeur, you help
          with homework, you're a nurse when
          we're sick ... ok, I get it.
          You're right, Mom, I could name
          twenty. Sorry.

                         122

                    MOM (O.S.)
          Thank you.

Lauren stands apologetically.

                    LAUREN
          I'll just come home after the game.

                    MOM (O.S.)
          I didn't say you couldn't go. I
          just thought a little appreciation
          would be nice.

As Lauren looks at her mother, a genuine appreciative
smile creases her face.

                    LAUREN
          Thanks.

                    MOM (O.S.)
          There's a twenty under the vase by
          the door. Emergency money.

                    LAUREN
          Thanks, Mom. You're the best. And
          Mom, I'll earn it. I promise.

Lauren races out.

                                        END

PAIGE & DAD (O.S.)   *"CLIQUED OFF"*

[Note: In this scene, Paige's main job is believable **listening**]

INT. DINING ROOM   NIGHT

An excited and animated PAIGE stands waiting for her Dad to get off the phone so she can tell him the news.

>   DAD (O.S.)
>   Sorry, honey.   What is it?

>   PAIGE
>   (excited)
>   Ok. There's this group at school,
>   and they are like the coolest girls
>   in the class, and they have invited
>   ME to join their group, and ....

>   DAD (O.S.)
>   (interrupting)
>   Who are they again?

>   PAIGE
>   Hannah, Sylvia, and Tiffany.
>   Anyway, I can join them, I can go
>   to their parties, wear their lip
>   shade....finally. But I need to
>   buy some things, the little skirt,
>   the pink shoes with the red heels
>   ...I really need them to like me.

>   DAD (O.S.)
>   Aren't these the same girls that
>   you said were snooty to you and
>   your friends?

>   PAIGE
>   Not anymore.   I saw them at the
>   mall and they invited me to join
>   them.   Ok, I bought their stuff at
>   the food court, but they like me!
>   So, can I buy the things I need?

>   DAD (O.S.)
>   Well, you can, *(she silently
>   cheers)* but let me ask you:
>   First, if they accept you or don't
>   accept you as fast as turning on a
>   faucet, do you trust it? Will you
>   be comfortable with them, or always
>   on edge, relying on money to save
>   you?
>   (more)

                    DAD (Cont'd)
          Do you have to drop the friends
          you've had for years just to be
          their friend? And second, it seems
          to be important that THEY like you.
          Do you like you? It's more
          important that you do.
          Think about it. The money is on
          my dresser.

She heads off, less excited than before. She turns back
to Dad.

                    PAIGE
          Dad? Would Mom have joined them?

                    DAD (O.S.)
          No. Your mom was a very confident
          woman.

She nods her head, then walks away very slowly.

                                        END

BONUS SCENE

The Bonus "You-Write" Scene

By now you might be saying to yourself _"I could write a scene like that"_.

Well, let's see.

I'll set up the parameters, you fill in the dialog.

How about this:

A girl is in an elevator, just about to close the door when a guy that she doesn't know runs up and jumps in.

The guy presses several buttons and the doors close.

He looks at her; she's uncomfortable, but not impolite.

Later, the elevator stops between floors.

After some discussion between the two, and before anyone panics, the elevator starts and the two continue on to their respective floor.

So…. does she get mad at him for pushing all the buttons (possibly causing the delay)? Is he the guy who delivers mail on all the floors or is he just an annoying guy pushing buttons?

Does she think he's cute?

Does he act macho and try to break through the door? Or does he take advantage of the situation and flirt with her?

When it finally opens, are they glad, or would they have liked to stay a little longer?

Let's see. Write in the dialog spaces on the next pages.

INT. LOBBY AND ELEVATOR - DAY   *"Bonus"*

LOREN is standing in the elevator waiting (hoping) for it
to close when GRADY runs in as it's closing.

                         GRADY
            Whew, just made it. Hi.

                         LOREN
            Hello.

He starts pushing buttons, about 10 in all.

                         LOREN

                         GRADY

                         LOREN

                         GRADY

                         LOREN

The elevator STOPS!

                         GRADY

                         LOREN

                         GRADY

Suddenly the elevator jolts and comes back to life. They
are hesitant to push the button for their floor again,
but finally they do and it moves.

                    LOREN

                    GRADY

                    LOREN

It's her floor. The door opens and she begins to step
out. As the door closes, she puts her hand to stop it,
looks back at him and says…..

                    LOREN

                    GRADY

The door closes again, maybe forever. Maybe not.

"*Characters are stuck with the actor who plays them.*"

- Jason Robards

COMMERCIAL SCENES

RECYCLE PSA

SAM is taking out the trash, sees a plastic bottle in the bag and pulls it out. As Sam stands over the recycle bin with the bottle, he/she looks at camera…..

SAM

Why do I recycle? Ahh, I don't know.

Sam looks down at the trash and the recycle bin, then looks directly into camera…

SAM

Oh, yeah. Because I care about the Earth.

Sam slam-dunks the bottle into the recycle bin.

WRIGLEY'S DOUBLEMINT GUM

INT. SCHOOL HALLWAY DAY

John scans the hallway, then sneaks a look at camera.

> JOHN
>
> I'd like to tell you that the main reason I chew Wrigley's Doublemint is because I really like the way the mint makes my mouth feel. Or the way the taste lasts for hours. But you really want to know why I chew Doublemint?
> *(looks off, smiles, back to us)*
> Nicole.

He puts the gum into his mouth, walks toward her.

The New Zephyr

A student stands in front of the class with a lab coat and glasses in mid-speech...

STUDENT

..so in conclusion, though its aerodynamic design and 3.2 liter engine make the van more fuel efficient, it's important to remember that the side airbags and automatic braking system --- make it safer too. Thank you.

AVO: *Buying a new Zephyr won't make everyone in your family smarter. It will just seem that way.*

KIDS' CLIF BAR

Chris rushes into the kitchen, hurrying, packing up a backpack and getting ready for school. As he/she packs, Chris grabs a Kid's Clif Bar from the table and tells us….

                    CHRIS
          When I don't have time for
          breakfast…I just grab a
          Kid's CLIF BAR and go.

Chris zips up the backpack, throws it over his/her shoulder, smiles and exits downstage.

<u>RECYCLE PSA #2</u> (for camera)

A girl, STACY, walks to a recycle bin with a plastic water bottle, a newspaper and an empty soda can. She addresses camera...

                    STACY
        See this bottle? It'll probably
        become some cool sunglasses. See
        this newspaper? Maybe a Nancy
        Drew Mystery. This can? It's
        going to be ... the flip-top of a
        cell phone.
        How?

[She dumps them into a recycle bin...]

                    STACY

   Magic.

[She snaps her fingers near her cheeks and disappears.*]

*As soon as she snaps her fingers, the camera is cut. She exits frame. Camera holds frame and shoots a few more seconds. Cut.
If the frames cut precisely, on playback it will look as if she's disappeared when she snaps her fingers.

SNICKER DOODLES

Two friends sit back to back, bored out of their skulls. Jordan's mom calls from off-screen…

> MOM (O.S.)
> Hey, would you kids like some snicker-doodles?

> JORDAN
> (scoffs, then to P.J.)
> Hmff. Snicker-doodles. She still thinks I'm a child.

> P.J.
> Actually, I like snicker- doodles.

> JORDAN
> Yeah, well, sometimes she makes 'em with M&Ms, too.

> P.J.
> They're home-made!?!

> MOM (O.S.)
> Well?

> P.J.
> She can treat ME like a child all she wants!

> JORDAN
> You're right. Let's go.
> COMING!!!

They race out toward the kitchen, where Mom has fresh-baked cookies. The Duncan Hines box is prominent in the foreground.

JetBlue

Four bored-out-of-their-skulls students sit slumped as the (off-screen) teacher drones on…

                    Teacher
Students, tomorrow we will
begin Chapter 6, the
history …. of aviation.

The kids start to sit up at the word "aviation" and become interested.

                Teacher (cont'd)
Does anyone know anything
about aviation?

                    Student 1
Yeah! Orville and Wilbur
Wright invented the first
airplane.

                    Student 2
And their plane was called the
Kitty Hawk.

                    Student 3
Yeah, it only stayed up about
a minute, in North Carolina.

                    Student 4
Charles Lindberg was the first
to go across the ocean by
himself on a flight to Paris.

The students now just start talking amongst themselves…..

                    Student 1
We flew to New York last
summer in just 4 hours.

                    Student 2
We were on a plane once, and
we were flying through the
clouds, then all of a sudden
wham! The clouds opened into
bright light and we could
see the Rockies below us.

                    Student 3
We were flying into Los
Angeles once on the 4th of
July and you could see the
fireworks **below us** as we were
coming in..

                    Student 4
Fireworks from up above, that
is so cool.

                    Student 1
We had this flight one time,
it was at sunset, and the
entire sky was orange…

                    Student 4
We did that once when we were
flying west, and it lasted
like 2 hours!

                    Student 1
Did you ever get to see a
plane take off right over
the top of you, and………

The students continue talking amongst themselves
(adlib)……

AVO: *JetBlue.   Because flying… is cool.*

TARGET

A kid is sitting at the table doing homework when he/she sees Mom and gets inspired.

                    KID
Hey Mom, your hair isn't looking
so good. And I think I know the
problem: split ends. But you
know what? They have a shampoo
for that. At Target---let's go
get you some!
          (*closes up the books*)
And since we're going to be at
Target anyway, we might as well
check out that Ipod that's on
sale. No sense in making two
trips, right? I'll get your
keys.

The kid exits with an "I'm so clever" smile.

"A career is born in public, talent in privacy."

                              - Marilyn Monroe

Acknowledgements:

This book would not be even remotely possible without the help of Denise Loveday-Kane.

Also, big thanks to Cinda Adams, Brian Scott and Grady Beard of On Your Mark Studios in Los Angeles, Director Mary Lou Belli, Casting Director John McCarthy, and kids' agent Jeremy Apody in Hollywood.

The front and back cover design is the work of the talented Mr. Thomas Cain.

I would also like to thank Lisa Megquier and her drama students at Griffith High School in Indiana for their help in the very early stages; it's a pleasure to work with them.

And Robert Barker and the drama students at Trinity High School in Canoga Park, California who performed the scenes for me and were very encouraging. Three of them are featured on the cover.

And thank you to all of the casting directors and directors who've allowed me to play characters and tell stories for a living; it's a privilege to be in this business, and work with some of the most talented people on earth.

And to all of my young acting students, past and present, a huge thank-you. I learn something from you every class, and it's made me a better actor.

– Bo Kane

For more information on Bo Kane and his acting classes in Los Angeles, California, go to

www.BoKaneonline.com

"Don't make being a 'star' your goal. There are too many factors beyond your control. The goal is to be a working actor. Because the secret to success, in acting or anything else, is to put all of your passion and effort into your craft -- hoping for, but not worrying about success."

— Bo Kane

About the Author:

As an actor, Bo Kane has worked in television, films and commercials, most recently in shows such as *Dexter*, *FlashForward*, *Men Of A Certain Age*, *The Unit*, and films such as *The Ringer*, *Camouflage*, and *Man Of The House*. He began his career in the 80's, appearing in such films as *El Norte*, *Child's Play*, *The Phantom*, *What's Love Got To Do With It* (as Dick Clark) and in television shows such as *JAG*, *Melrose Place*, *The X-Files*, *Arli$$*, *General Hospital*, *The Magnificent Seven*, *Young & Restless*, and many others.

As a writer, Bo wrote the newspaper columns "Man's Eye View" for the Sun-Times News Group, and "Hollywood Hoosiers" for The Times. He is also the co-author of "The Wild World Of The Wilders", a tv series in development.

Bo has also worked on farms, in steel mills, as a newscaster for CBS affiliates, and for the U.S. Congress. He was the Head Coach for the Special Olympic Equestrian Team in the San Fernando Valley for many years, and coached the California team in the World Games.

Bo is a graduate of the University of Notre Dame.

Aside from his acting and writing career, Bo currently teaches kids' acting classes in Los Angeles.

He and his wife, Denise, have two children.

"Writing is what you do when you're ready, and acting is what you do when someone else is ready."

— Steve Martin

Made in the USA
Lexington, KY
07 June 2011